Revision Guide to Economics

for AS Level and A Level Year 1

Peter Cramp

© Anforme Ltd 2016
ISBN 978-1-78014-016-2
Images supplied by Shutterstock.com

Anforme Ltd, Stocksfield Hall, Stocksfield, Northumberland NE43 7TN.

Typeset by George Wishart & Associates, Whitley Bay.
Printed by Potts Print (UK) Ltd.

Contents

The first pages offer you advice on using this book. After this, you will find revision notes organised as shown below:

Paper 1 – Microeconomics

Paper 2 – Macroeconomics

Using this book

This book provides revision notes for AS-level Economics and the first year of a two-year A-level course. The material in it has been chosen to ensure that it covers the following AS-level specifications: AQA, Edexcel A and OCR. The majority of the material is common to all these specifications. Occasionally there is material which is only specified at AS-level by one or two of the exam boards and every attempt has been made to indicate where this is so. Almost all of the material in this book will be relevant to you if you are studying for A-level, whichever specification you are following. In many ways, it is good advice to study all of the material in the book, regardless of the context of your study – you can never know too much economic theory!

Microeconomics is examined in Paper 1 of both AS-level and A-level courses. The microeconomics content of this book follows a defined structure. It is important that you understand this structure:

Microeconomics – Structure	
Introductory concepts	Scarcity, factors of production, wants and needs, maximising behaviour, rationality, positive and normative economics, production possibilities.
Markets generally work well	Price Mechanism: Competitive markets allocate resources efficiently through the forces of supply and demand, setting the relative prices of goods.
Sometimes markets fail	Market failure occurs when markets fail to produce desirable outcomes, either because the allocation of resources is not efficient or because the outcome is unfair (there is a lack of equity).
This may justify government intervention	Governments may respond to market failure by intervening to improve the resource allocation or produce a more equitable outcome.
Government failure sometimes occurs	Government intervention is not always effective in achieving its aims. The costs of intervention may exceed the benefits, creating a loss of economic welfare. This is government failure.

Each of the microeconomics chapters in the book has a bar at the top showing the above structure and highlighting where the particular chapter fits into this structure. For example, Chapter 2 is about demand and supply analysis and is a building block in helping us to understand why markets generally work well and allocate resources efficiently. 'Markets generally work well' is therefore highlighted within the structure:

Chapter 2	Paper 1: Introductory concepts → **Markets generally work well** → Sometimes markets fail → This may justify government intervention → Government failure sometimes occurs
	Demand and supply analysis

If a particular chapter crosses over more than one bit of the structure, the relevant parts of the structure are all highlighted.

Macroeconomics is examined in Paper 2 of both AS-level and A-level courses. The notes for macroeconomics also follow a defined structure:

Macroeconomics – Structure	
Measuring the macroeconomy	The main four macroeconomic objectives (strong and sustainable growth, low unemployment, low and stable inflation and a satisfactory current account of the balance of payments) and how the corresponding indicators are measured.
How the macroeconomy works	The circular flow of income and aggregate supply/aggregate demand analysis.
Macroeconomic performance	Understanding the demand and supply side factors which influence performance with regard to the four main economic objectives. The difference between factors that affect the short run performance of the economy and the fundamental supply side determinants of long run performance.
International trade	The reasons for trade, comparative advantage theory, the pattern of trade, the balance of payments and policies to influence it, the determination of exchange rates.
Macroeconomic policy tools	Fiscal and monetary policies as ways of influencing aggregate demand and stabilising the economy. Supply side policy as a tool to influence trend growth and long term economic performance.

The chapter headings also work in the same way in the second section of the book as they did in the first. For example, Chapter 14 on the circular flow of income and aggregate demand is about how the macroeconomy works so this is highlighted accordingly.

Chapter **14**	**Paper 2:** Measuring the macroeconomy → **How the macroeconomy works** → Macroeconomic performance → Macroeconomic policy tools
	The circular flow of income and aggregate demand (AD)

I wish you good luck with your revision programme and your exams.

Peter Cramp

Paper 1: Introductory concepts → Markets generally work well → Sometimes markets fail → This may justify government intervention → Government failure sometimes occurs

Introduction to economics

Overview

One of the first questions students ask when they start a course in economics is why is there a need to study the subject? The simple answer is that there is a **basic economic problem** – there are only a limited number of resources available to satisfy our needs and wants. Thus economists must attempt to reconcile this problem of **scarce resources** and **infinite desires**.

Needs and wants

Man's physical needs are limited. They include food, water, clothing, warmth and shelter. Economists assume that man's wants are, in contrast, unlimited – for example, even a person who owns five luxury houses is likely to want more.

Factors of production (economic resources)

The **finite resources** used to produce output can be divided into four groups. Collectively, they are called the **factors of production**:

● **Land** – the natural resources on the planet. These include produce obtained from oceans and rivers, and as a result of a favourable climate. Minerals extracted from the planet, such as diamonds and aluminium, are also classified as land. Some natural resources are **renewables** (such as wind) others are **non-renewable resources** (such as fossil fuels).

● **Labour** – human resources used to produce goods and services. In the UK, there are around 32 million workers involved in the production process.

● **Capital** – items used by labour in the production process. Examples include factories, machines, roads and computers. All these capital items allow the production of goods and services in future time periods.

● **Enterprise** – the individual, or group of individuals, prepared to take a risk and combine the three other factors of production.

Each factor of production earns a reward, known as a factor payment. The factor payments are:

Factor	Payment
Land	Rent
Labour	Wages and salaries
Capital	Interest
Enterprise	Profit

The purpose of economic activity

The central purpose of economic activity is to combine factors of production (resources) to produce **output** for consumption. By satisfying needs and wants, the output produced generates **satisfaction or utility** and thereby increases **economic welfare**. Output can be subdivided into goods and services. Further subdivisions are possible. For example, goods can be either durable (such as furniture) or non-durable (such as food).

Economists take a fairly broad view of economic activity. Housework and DIY could be included, for example. They involve combining resources to produce valuable output, even if that output is not traded.

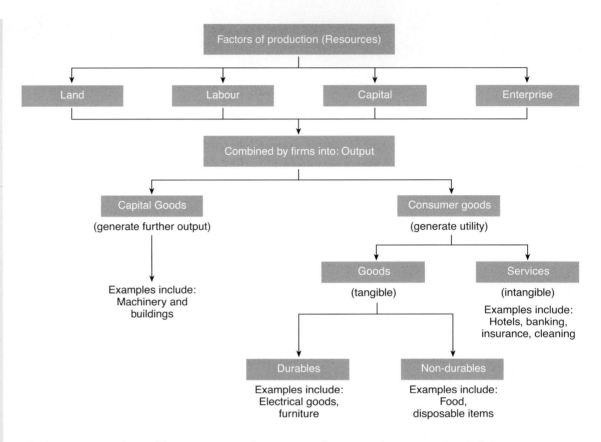

Scarcity and the economic problem

The basic **economic problem** is scarcity of resources. This occurs because society's finite resources are scarce relative to infinite needs and wants.

The basic economic problem means decisions must be made by society, or by individuals, about how to allocate resources. This involves answering three key questions:

1. What goods and services are to be produced?
2. How are they produced?
3. For whom are they produced?

Economic agents

The main agents (participants) in the economy are individuals such as **consumers** or **workers**, the **firms** who produce output and the **government**. All these agents have decisions to make regarding resource allocation.

Market economies

A market is any place in which a buyer and seller interact. This does not imply that the buyer and seller meet face to face (consider the market for items sold on e-Bay, for example). In a market economy, resources are allocated through the interaction of individuals and firms. The role of the government is limited to things like protecting people's rights to their property and issuing notes and coins.

In market theory, it is assumed that economic agents adopt **maximising behaviour**:

● Consumers try to maximise their satisfaction or utility from consumption, subject to the constraint of the income available to them.

● Workers try to maximise their income, subject to the constraint of wanting to enjoy leisure time.

● Firms try to maximise profits.

It is also assumed that economic agents are **rational**. If I choose to spend £20 on watching a football match rather than going out for a meal, it is because I gain more satisfaction or utility from the football match. The assumption of rationality rules out the possibility that I would have enjoyed the meal more than the football match and have simply made a mistake.

Here is how the three key questions posed by the problem of scarcity are answered in a market economy:

● The question of "**What goods and services are to be produced?**" is answered by the interaction of supply and demand in the price mechanism. There will be high demand for goods that generate high levels of satisfaction or utility. High demand forces the price of these goods up, giving an incentive to profit maximising producers to extend the supply of them.

● The question of "**How are they produced?**" is largely answered by firms. Firms are likely to seek the lowest cost methods of production in order to maximise profits.

● The distribution of income determines the answer to "**For whom are they produced?**". Those with more income will consume more goods than those with less income.

Alternative views of consumer behaviour

There are **alternative views of consumer behaviour** which question the assumption of rationality. We may get more realistic models of consumer behaviour by considering factors such as:

● The influence of other people's behaviour. The wish to conform to expectations and be accepted as part of a group may influence what consumers choose to buy. One application of this idea is in understanding fads and fashions in consumer demand.

● The importance of habitual behaviour. Buying things out of habit can sometimes be useful for consumers. Buying the same things each week at the supermarket saves time, for instance, but could lead consumers not to look at substitute products which might carry more utility. At other times, habit influences consumers in an unhelpful way. Many consumers would like to make more healthy choices in their diet, for example, or to give up smoking but find existing habits impossible to break even though those habits might not be maximising consumer utility.

● Consumer weakness at computation. Most observers would accept that consumers are not really able to perform the complex calculations which would be necessary for consumers to spend their limited income in a way which maximised their utility. Consumer behaviour is influenced by many factors such as impulse, habit and rules-of-thumb (e.g. never to pay more than £7 for a bottle of wine or to buy as much of the weekly grocery shop through 'special offers' as possible). There is also significant evidence that consumers place too much importance on factors in the present (such as the pleasure gained from eating unhealthy foods) and tend to ignore the future (such as the long-term health consequences).

These alternative views of consumer behaviour are only explicitly required at AS-level for Edexcel A, but are developed much further by some exam boards in A-level Year 2, notably in AQA's section on **behavioural economics**.

Mixed economies

Most economies in the world are mixed economies. This means that both markets and governments play a role in resource allocation. Governments intervene when markets fail to produce desirable outcomes (in other words, governments intervene to overcome market failures). The government sector of the economy is known as the **public sector**, while economic activity produced by other economic agents constitutes the **private sector**. The size of the public sector varies from one economy to another, but in the UK the government accounts for around 40% of economic activity.

Command economies

In command economies, the key decisions regarding resource allocation are all made by the government. The government decides what to produce and determines the price of goods. Equally, firms and hence their capital equipment are owned by the state rather than by individuals, thus the government decides what to produce. The government is also likely to dictate wages thus effectively deciding the question of "for whom are goods produced?".

Advantages and disadvantages of market and command economies

The **advantages and disadvantages of market and command economies** (*this section is only explicitly required for the Edexcel A specification at AS-level*)

While market economies are prone to market failure, the experience of command economies suggests that there is a large potential for government failure. This helps to understand why there are few modern command economies, although Cuba and North Korea can be argued to fall into this category. China once had a command economy before its market reforms. Some advantages and disadvantages of command economies are shown below (these can essentially be reversed for the advantages and disadvantages of market economies)

Advantages of command economies	Disadvantages of command economies
They can achieve a more equal distribution of income (sometimes argued to be fairer)	A lack of individual economic incentives can lead to a lack of wealth creation
They are less prone to economic cycles and therefore to problems such as recession. They may also be able to prevent high levels of unemployment	Command economies do not respond to market signals. This can lead to excess supply of some goods and shortages of others.
Governments may be able to direct resources to where they are most socially useful, rather than to where they generate profit.	Governments may make choices which fail to maximise welfare, such as amassing weapons but failing to produce enough food.

Those who believe in market economics tend to admire theories such as Adam Smith's **invisible hand theory**. Smith argued that under certain conditions, the interaction of self-interested firms, consumers and workers would produce an efficient allocation of resources (maximising utility) without the need for any government intervention. Smith's best known work is the *Wealth of Nations 1776*.

Supporters of command economies often adhere to the theories of Karl Marx, who co-wrote the *Communist Manifesto* with Friedrich Engels in 1848. Marx argued that free market economies contained the seeds of their own destruction because the gap between the wealth and income of businessmen (the owners of capital) and those of the workers would grow until the workers overthrew the system through a revolution. Workers (known as the proletariat) would choose to put in place a system with no private property in a command economy.

Friedrich von Hayek in his work *The Road to Serfdom* (1944) warned of "the danger of tyranny that inevitably results from government control of economic decision making through central planning."

Opportunity cost – the next best alternative foregone

The problem of scarce resources means that choices have to be made. As discussed in the previous section, this is true for individuals, firms and governments who all have to make decisions about how to allocate resources.

- An individual does not have an unlimited income and must therefore make economic choices on a daily basis. This could be whether to buy a new phone or a games console. Workers must also decide if it is worth sacrificing leisure time so they can earn extra income to raise their standard of living.

- Firms may have to decide whether to use profits to invest in new machinery or to increase dividends to shareholders.

- Governments cannot spend infinite amounts of money on public services. They may be faced with difficult decisions, such as whether to increase spending on the National Health Service or on Education.

Such choices nearly always involve a cost. For example, the decision to purchase the phone means that the games console will have to be given up. This is known as **opportunity cost** and is defined as **the next best alternative foregone**.

Economic goods and free goods

Economic goods are those that use scarce resources when they are produced, and therefore carry an opportunity cost. The only major resource on earth that is not scarce is the air that we breathe. This is called a **free good**.

Production possibility frontiers

A **production possibility frontier** (PPF) illustrates what an economy can produce using the resources of land, labour, capital and enterprise. It is useful in explaining the concept of **opportunity cost**. Consider the example of an economy that allocates all its resources to providing either manufactured goods or services. This is illustrated in Figure 1.1.

Figure 1.1

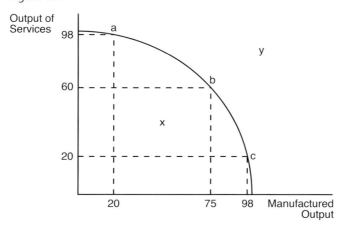

● Points a, b, and c all lie on the PPF and show maximum production when all economic resources are **fully employed** and used **efficiently**.

● Point x lies within the frontier and illustrates a situation where the factors of production are not fully employed and/or are being used **inefficiently**.

● Point y is not yet attainable given the current level of resources in the economy.

The production possibility frontier can be used to illustrate **opportunity cost**. The concave shape of the frontier indicates that the opportunity cost of manufactured goods in terms of services increases as more manufactured goods are produced.

If the economy were to **specialise** in producing manufactured goods, increasing output from 20 units to 75 units would lead to a relatively small fall in the production of services from 98 units to 60 units. The **opportunity cost** of the 55 unit increase in manufactured output is the 38 units of services that have been foregone.

Specialising even further, and increasing manufactured output from 75 units to 98 units, leads to a relatively large fall in the provision of services from 60 to 20 units. The **opportunity cost** of this small 23 unit rise in manufactured output is the 40 units of services that have been foregone.

This increasing opportunity cost can be explained by the fact that not all resources are equally suited to the provision of manufactured goods and services. The factors of production used in increasing manufactured output from 75 to 98 units are far better suited to the provision of services and this explains why the output of manufactured goods only increases by a relatively small amount.

Shifts in the production possibility frontier

In Figure 1.2, the PPF shifts outwards in parallel direction. This could have been caused by:

● An increase in the quantity of the factors of production – the shift may have originated from the discovery of new energy supplies, an increase in the active workforce or investment in new machinery.

● Improvements in efficiency or new technology – if there is an increase in the productivity of factors of production this will allow more output to be produced. The IT revolution of the last few years has caused the PPFs of many economies to shift outwards.

Figure 1.2

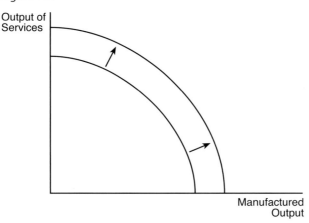

An improvement in new technology will not always cause a parallel shift in the PPF. For example, a new computerised production process will only impact on the manufacturing sector. The productive potential of the service sector will remain unchanged. This will lead to a shift in the PPF as shown in Figure 1.3.

Figure 1.3

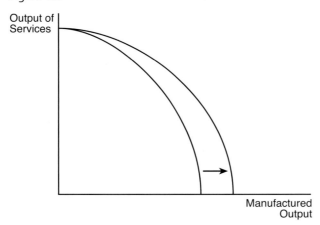

Specialisation (the division of labour)

Specialisation occurs at many different levels. Individuals may specialise in a particular occupation (Economics teaching, for example). Firms specialise (as Microsoft does in computer software). There are particular regional specialisations, such as pottery in Stoke-on-Trent, although such specialisations are increasingly under threat from international competition. Finally there are international specialisations. China could be argued to specialise in manufacturing, for instance, while the UK has a strength in financial services.

Specialisation is a means of avoiding the need to be self-sufficient, thereby increasing output and living standards. We would all be materially worse off if we had to make our own clothes, build our own houses and grow or hunt our own food. It would be difficult to satisfy our basic needs, let alone to cater for the many desires that are satisfied in modern economies.

The specific **advantages of specialisation** are that it allows greater output for the following reasons:

● Workers can be assigned to tasks to which they are well suited.

● Workers 'learn by doing' and efficiency improves through experience.

● Production line methods save time changing tools.

● Production line methods may make it cost effective to provide specialist capital equipment for workers.

The IT revolution has caused the PPFs of many economies to shift outwards.

On the other hand, there are **disadvantages of specialisation**, such as:

● Boredom for workers engaged in repetitive tasks, which may in turn make them less productive.

● Regions or countries that specialise are dependent on other regions or countries for obtaining other products and services. This could cause problems in the event of trade disputes or wars between countries.

For specialisation to work well, it is vital that there is an **efficient means of exchanging products and services** with those who have other specialisations. The market economy serves this role well.

The functions of money

The functions of money *(this section is only explicitly required for Edexcel A at AS-level)*

The existence of money is vital for providing an efficient means of exchanging goods and services and thus allowing for specialisation.

This is primarily because money functions as a **medium of exchange** and is accepted as payment for goods and services, thus removing the inefficiency of a barter economy in which a successful trade requires a **double coincidence of wants** (each of the two agents involved in a trade wishes to buy exactly what the other is selling).

Other functions of money include:

● **Measure of value** – prices can be used to compare the value of two goods.

● **Store of value** – savings can be held in monetary form.

● **Standard of deferred payment** – credit agreements such as 'buy now, pay later' are possible.

The functions of money are impaired by inflation, which erodes the real value of money over time. Unpredictable inflation also makes price comparisons more difficult, while hyperinflation may even prevent money carrying out its most basic function of being accepted as a medium of exchange.

Normative and positive economics

There are two types of economic statements:

- **Positive Statements** – an objective statement. It is a statement of fact or a testable hypothesis (that is, a claim for which evidence to support or reject the claim can be gathered).

- **Normative Statements** – an opinion or view (in other words, a 'value judgement' about what ought to be, or should be, done).

For example, the UK's emissions of CO_2 are around 10% of that of the United States. This is a **positive statement** as it objectively describes a situation in the economy. The claim that an increase in duty on petrol would help to reduce emissions is also a **positive statement**. Support for the claim could be found in economic theory and empirical ('real world') evidence of what has happened in the past or in other countries when duty on petrol has been raised.

If an economist argued that the US should dramatically reduce its emissions; this is a **normative statement** as it expresses an opinion.

Economics as a social science

Economics as a social science *(this section is only explicitly required for Edexcel A and AQA)*

Economics is usually regarded as a social science, along with other subjects such as Psychology and Sociology.

In some respects Economics is similar to natural sciences such as Physics, Biology and Chemistry. The scientific method involves constructing hypotheses about how the world works and gathering empirical evidence against which they can be tested. Economists often build models which yield testable hypotheses. For example, supply and demand analysis models the interaction of consumers and firms in markets and leads to testable hypotheses such as that a rise in the price of a good will lead to a contraction of demand for it.

However, there are key differences between Economics and the natural sciences:

- Natural scientists can often conduct experiments under controlled laboratory conditions, where all variables except one are held constant. This occurs, for example, when chemists observe the effect of adding more of just one chemical to a given compound. By contrast, when the price of a good rises, many other factors affecting its demand such as the level of consumer incomes, may also be changing. Economists make the *ceteris paribus* **assumption**, meaning all other things being equal or held constant, but they cannot directly gather evidence of the effect of a single variable such as the price of a good changing.

- Economists and other social scientists study human behaviour. Humans make choices in a way which is not true of the subjects of the natural sciences. When choosing between courses of action, economic agents must make judgements about their desirability. They may respond to economic incentives (self-interest) and also be influenced by moral and political considerations. When building models, economists have to make simplifying assumptions about the choices of economic agents, such as the assumption of maximising behaviour on the part of economic agents.

- When making choices, the behaviour of economic agents may not be entirely predictable or consistent in the way that the behaviour of, say, chemicals is. Thus, given the same economic incentives on two different occasions the same individual may well react in a different way.

Factors such as those above make the gathering of evidence to test hypotheses more difficult in economics than in the natural sciences.

Chapter

2

Paper 1: Introductory concepts → **Markets generally work well** → Sometimes markets fail → This may justify government intervention → Government failure sometimes occurs

Demand and supply analysis

Effective demand

Demand in economics must always be **effective**. Only when a consumer's desire to buy something is backed up by a **willingness** and an **ability** to pay for it do we speak of demand. For example, many people would be willing to buy a luxury sports car, but their demand would not be effective if they did not have the means to do so. They must have sufficient **purchasing power**.

Demand curves

Demand is defined as the **quantity** of a good or service that consumers are **willing and able to buy at a given price in a given time period**. For most goods there is an **inverse relationship** between the quantity demanded and the good's own price. This is illustrated in Figure 2.1.

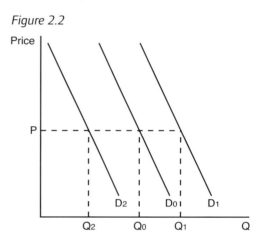

Figure 2.1

Figure 2.2

- A **change in the price** of the **good itself** causes a **movement** along the demand curve. For example in Figure 2.1, a **rise in price** from P to P_1 causes a **contraction** along the demand curve. Conversely, a fall in price from P to P_2 leads to an **expansion** in quantity demanded. These movements along the demand curve are usually caused by shifts in the supply curve, although they might also be caused by the imposition of specific prices by the government.

- A change in one of the **conditions of demand** will lead to a **shift** in the demand curve. This is illustrated in Figure 2.2. When the demand curve shifts to the right (D_0 to D_1) more is demanded at each and every price (Q_0 to Q_1). When demand shifts to the left (D_0 to D_2), there is a fall in demand for the product at each price level (Q_0 to Q_2).

Shifting demand curves – the conditions of demand

A change in any of the following conditions of demand will cause the demand curve to shift. However, remember: never shift the demand curve when the price of the good itself changes.

Conditions of demand include:

1. **Real income** measures the quantity of goods and services that a consumer can afford to buy. An **increase in real income** will cause the demand curve to shift to the **right** for the vast majority of goods that are classed as **normal**. However, some goods are **inferior** – this is where an increase in real income will cause demand to shift to the **left**. Examples of inferior goods may include rice, potatoes, tobacco and bus travel. An increase in income will cause the demand for bus travel to fall, as commuters switch to superior modes of transport such as private motor cars or rail services. The impact of a change of income on demand is analysed further in Chapter 3 when we look at **income elasticity of demand**.

2. **Prices of other goods – Substitutes and Complements**

Substitute goods or services are those in **competitive demand** that satisfy a similar need or want. Examples include different brands of soap powders, or types of crisps or soft drinks.

● A fall in the price of a substitute good will cause demand to shift to the left. If there is a fall in local rail fares (a substitute for bus travel), demand for train services will increase, but demand for bus travel will shift to the left.

Complementary goods or services are those goods and services that are often consumed together. They are said to be in **joint demand**. Examples include tennis racquets and tennis balls and package holidays and travel insurance.

● A fall in the price of a **complementary good** will cause the demand curve to shift to the right. If there is a fall in the price of new and second hand cars, the demand for these products will expand, and the demand for petrol (a complementary good) will shift to the right.

3. **Tastes and preferences** – tastes can be volatile, and often lead to a change in demand. Fluctuations in consumer tastes can lead to big variations in demand at each price. This is particularly true for products that are fashionable for a very short period while there is a craze to purchase them. These goods are called **fads**.

   Standard demand theory assumes that consumer preferences are fixed – meaning that one person's preferences do not affect those of others. This is now being questioned. In many markets, the views of some consumers have an impact on the preferences of other consumers (either positively or negatively) – these feedback effects can mean that demand for certain goods and services becomes volatile and difficult to predict.

4. **Interest rates** – the level of interest rates affects the demand for many items, particularly 'big ticket' household durable goods (TVs, consumer electronics and dishwashers) and items typically purchased on **credit** (cars, home improvements and holidays).

   A rise in interest rates will reduce demand. Higher interest rates increase the incentive for consumers to postpone consumption and save their money instead. Higher rates will also increase the cost of loan repayments and discourage consumers from undertaking a purchase. Changes in interest rates also affect **consumer confidence** and therefore influence the willingness of consumers to commit themselves to major items of spending.

5. **Population changes** – a rise in population will shift the demand for most goods to the right. However, the age structure of the population is also important. The UK has an **ageing population** and, inevitably, the demand for products such as pensions, nursing homes and stair lifts will shift to the right.

6. **Advertising and Marketing** – a successful advertising or marketing campaign will shift demand to the right. This in itself makes the **price elasticity of demand** (see Chapter 3) for the product more inelastic.

Ceteris paribus

It is important to remember that the demand curve is drawn assuming **ceteris paribus**; that is, 'all other things being equal'. A change in any of the **conditions of demand** will result in a **shift** in the demand curve. Only a change in the **price of the good** itself will lead to a **movement** along the curve.

Why do demand curves slope downwards?

The main reason that demand curves slope downwards from left to right is because a fall in price makes the good cheaper relative to substitutes (this is called the **substitution effect**). The fall in price also increases the consumer's purchasing power and may encourage them to buy more of the good (this is called the **income effect**).

We can also understand the downwards slope of the demand curve through the concept of **diminishing marginal utility**. The more of a good consumed, the less utility is derived from each marginal (additional) unit of it. Rationally, therefore consumers are only prepared to buy more of a good at a lower price. I might be prepared to pay £1 for my first chocolate bar, but only 60p for a second, for example, because I place a lower value on the second chocolate bar as I am not as hungry already having consumed one. Because market demand curves are derived by adding the demand of individual consumers together, the principle of diminishing marginal utility suggests demand curves will be downward sloping. The principle of the concept of diminishing marginal utility is only explicitly required at AS level for the Edexcel A specification.

Exceptions to the law of demand

For a small number of goods, the demand curve may slope upwards from left to right.

Veblen goods – A fall in the price of a luxury product that is consumed for ostentatious reasons may result in a fall in demand. This is because as the price of the product falls it loses some of its snob appeal and kudos and consumers will switch to more expensive and exclusive products.

Giffen goods are very inferior products on which low income consumers spend a high proportion of their income. Basic foodstuffs in developing countries, such as rice, may be an example. When the price rises, consumers may not have enough income left to buy more expensive items of food that previously provided some variety in their diet. Instead, they buy more rice.

Supply curves

Supply is defined as the **willingness and ability** of producers to supply output onto a market at a **given price in a given period of time**.

There is usually a **positive relationship between supply and price**. As prices rise it becomes more profitable for existing firms to increase output and supply may be boosted further by the entry of new firms into the industry.

A change in the **own price of the good** (caused by a shift in the demand curve) results in a **movement along the supply curve**. A fall in price causes a **contraction**. A rise in price causes an **expansion**. This is illustrated in Figure 2.3. A change in one of the **conditions of supply** causes a shift in the supply curve. When the supply curve shifts to the right more goods are supplied at each and every price. This is shown in Figure 2.4.

Figure 2.3

Figure 2.4

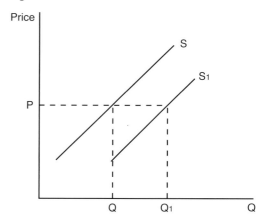

Conditions of supply

Just as with the demand curve, remember that a change in the price of the good itself does not shift the supply curve. However, the supply curve does shift when any of the following **conditions of supply** change:

1. **Prices of factors of production** – raw materials, components and wage levels. A fall in the price of paper would shift the supply curve for a newspaper producer to the right as more output can be supplied at each price. In contrast, for a haulage company, higher fuel costs would cause supply to shift to the left because fuel is an essential raw material.

2. **Productivity of factors** – an improvement in labour productivity means that each worker will be able to produce a higher level of output. This will reduce **unit labour costs** and shift the supply curve to the right. The efficiency gains may be partly passed onto the consumers in the form of lower prices.

3. **Indirect taxes or subsidies** – the introduction of VAT or additional excise duties on a good will shift the supply curve to the left. This is because taxes add to the costs faced by a producer. The supply curve of the airline industry has shifted to the left following the introduction of air passenger duty.

    A **subsidy** encourages a producer to increase production. The grant or payment from the government will lower a firm's costs of production and shift the supply curve to the right. The supply curve of many agricultural commodities has been shifted to the left following a reduction in subsidies from the European Union.

4. **Producer decisions** – the aims of a business can affect its supply decision. For example, if a firm switched from **revenue maximisation** to **profit maximisation** this would cause the supply curve to shift to the left.

5. **Technological advances** such as the developments in robotics and information technology reduce the costs of production and shift the supply curve to the right.

6. **Prices of substitutes** – a rise in the price of a substitute will cause supply to shift to the left. Suppose the price of parsnips rose, this would encourage farmers to increase the production of this particular root vegetable and reduce the supply of others such as carrots and turnips.

7. **Entry of new firms into an industry** – the entrance of new firms into an industry shifts the supply curve to the right and puts downward pressure on the market price.

Market equilibrium

Market equilibrium occurs when the **market clears**, with supply equal to demand. This is shown in Figure 2.5(a) with the equilibrium price at P and the quantity traded at Q. The significance of the equilibrium price is that consumers are able to buy exactly the amount they wish to purchase at that price, while suppliers are able to sell the amount that they wish to sell. Consequently, no participant in the market has an incentive to change their behaviour: market equilibrium is a **state of rest**, with no forces acting to bring about a change in price. Market equilibrium will only be disturbed if one of the conditions of supply or demand changes leading to a shift in the relevant curve.

When there is a situation of excess supply or demand, the market is said to be in disequilibrium. Market **forces** then act to push the market back towards equilibrium.

Market forces

Figure 2.5(a)

Equilibrium

Figure 2.5(b)

Excess Supply

Figure 2.5(c)

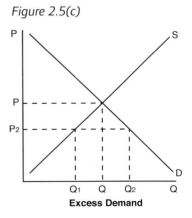

Excess Demand

Excess supply: In Figure 2.5(b), when prices are at P_1 there is **excess supply** (quantity supplied Q_2 is greater than quantity demanded Q_1) and firms will be forced to reduce prices in order to shed stocks. There will be an expansion along the demand curve and a contraction in supply until a new equilibrium is established at a lower market price P.

Excess demand: In Figure 2.5(c), when the price is at P_2 there is **excess demand** (quantity demanded Q_2 is greater than quantity supplied Q_1) and prices will be forced upwards as there is a **shortage** of the product. This causes an expansion along the supply curve and a contraction in demand until equilibrium is, once again, restored at price P.

The effect of a shift in demand

Ceteris paribus, **a shift in the demand curve to the right**, will raise prices **and** expand the quantity supplied.

Figure 2.6

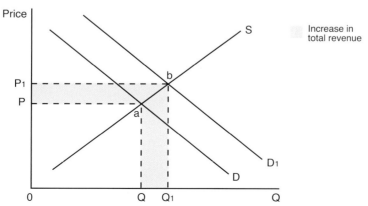

In Figure 2.6 it is assumed that the market for a normal good is in equilibrium at price P and quantity Q. Suppose there is now an increase in **consumers' real income** that causes the demand curve to shift to the **right** from D to D_1. At the **original price** P there is a **shortage** (a-b). This shortage will cause prices to be bid upwards and this will result in an **expansion or extension** along the supply curve until a new equilibrium is established at a **higher price** (P_1) and a **higher level of output** (Q_1). The more **inelastic the supply curve**, **the larger** the increase in price and the **smaller** the rise in output.

When **demand shifts to the right** the firm experiences a **rise in total revenue** (price x quantity). The shaded area in Figure 2.7 shows the increase in total revenue. At price P, the original level of total revenue is equal to 0PaQ. Following the outward shift in demand, the new level of total revenue is $0P_1bQ_1$.

Although there is a rise in total revenue it cannot be immediately assumed that a firm's profit will rise. This is because there is also a **rise in the firm's total costs** as output has increased from Q to Q_1. In this instance the **effect on profit is therefore ambiguous**, since both revenue and costs have increased. It is impossible to tell accurately whether profits will rise or fall.

Figure 2.7

Price

P₁
P

0   Q   Q₁   Q

Increase in
total revenue

The effect of a shift in supply

Ceteris paribus, **a shift in the supply curve to the right**, will reduce prices **and** expand the quantity demanded.

In Figure 2.8, the market is in equilibrium at price P and quantity Q. Suppose there is now a technological advance which causes the **supply curve** to shift to the **right** from S to S_1. At the **original price** P there will be a **surplus** (a-b). Suppliers will lower their prices to reduce stocks and this will result in an **expansion** along the demand curve until a new equilibrium is established at a **lower price** (P_1) and a **higher level of output** (Q_1). The more inelastic the demand curve the **larger** the fall in price and **smaller** the increase in output.

Figure 2.8

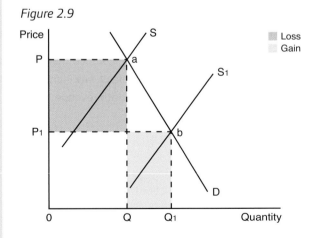

When **supply shifts to the right** the impact on total revenue depends on the price elasticity of demand (see Chapter 3). In Figure 2.9, demand is inelastic. At the original price P, total revenue was equal to the area OPaQ. Following the outward shift in supply, the new area of total revenue is equal to OP_1bQ_1. The fall in price from P to P_1 results in a fall in total revenue **because the area of loss exceeds the area of gain**.

The effect on profit in this case is clear-cut, as there is also a **rise in the firm's total costs** because output has increased from Q to Q_1. As the firm's revenue has decreased while its costs have increased, its **profit will fall**.

Figure 2.9

Price elasticity of demand (PED)

Price elasticity of demand measures the responsiveness of **quantity demanded** to a change in the good's **own price**. The formula for the calculation of PED is:

$$\text{Price elasticity of demand (PED)} = \frac{\text{\% change in the quantity demanded of good X}}{\text{\% change in the price of good X}}$$

Calculating PED

Consider the following demand schedule for buses in a city centre.

Price (average fare)	Quantity of passengers per week
100p	1,000
60p	1,300
30p	2,275

Suppose the current average fare is 100p, what is the PED if fares are cut to 60p?

The **percentage change in quantity demanded** is equal to:

● the change in demand 300 (1,300 - 1,000) divided by the original level of demand 1000. To obtain a percentage this must be multiplied by 100. The full calculation is (300 ÷ 1,000) x 100 = 30%.

The **percentage change in price** is equal to:

● the fall in price 40p (100p - 60p) divided by the original price 100p. To obtain a percentage this must be multiplied by 100. The full calculation is (-40 ÷ 100) x 100 = -40%.

These two figures can then be inserted in to the formula with 30% ÷ -40% = **-0.75**.

Let us now consider the PED when the average fare is cut from 60p to 30p.

The **percentage change in quantity demanded** is equal to:

● the change in demand 975 (2,275 - 1,300) divided by the original level of demand 1,300. To obtain a percentage this must be multiplied by 100. The full calculation is (975 ÷ 1,300) x 100 = 75%.

The **percentage change in price** is equal to:

● the fall in price 30p (60p - 30p) divided by the original price 60p. To obtain a percentage this must be multiplied by 100. The full calculation is (-30 ÷ 60) x 100 = -50%.

These two figures can then be inserted into the formula with 75% ÷ 50% = **1.5**.

There are some important points worth remembering when calculating PED:

● PED is a **real number**, not a percentage or fraction.

● The PED will **vary along a demand curve** and will depend on the **direction of the price change**. For example if the average bus fare were to rise from 60p to 100p, the PED would be 0.34. The percentage change in quantity demanded is 23% while the percentage change in price is 67%. When the price fell from 100p to 60p the elasticity was 0.75.

● The PED for all **normal goods** will be **negative** because a rise in price will cause a fall in quantity demanded and vice versa. When, however, we analyse the significance of the PED the **sign is often ignored**.

What do the elasticity figures tell us?	**Elasticity value**	**Description**	**Meaning**
	Zero	Totally inelastic	Demand is completely unresponsive to price changes
	Between zero and one	Inelastic	Demand responds less than proportionately to price changes
	One	Unitary elasticity	Demand responds proportionately to a change in price
	Between one and infinity	Elastic	Demand responds more than proportionately to a price change
	Infinity	Perfectly elastic	Demand is completely sensitive to the price. Any price increase causes demand to fall to zero

Diagrams for different PED values

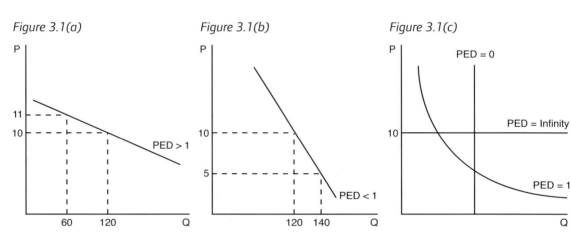

Figure 3.1(a)   Figure 3.1(b)   Figure 3.1(c)

● In Figure 3.1(a), the price rise from 10p to 11p results in a 50% fall in quantity demanded, which is greater than the 10% rise in price. The PED = 5. As this is greater than 1, the good is **elastic**.

● In Figure 3.1(b), the fall in price from 10p to 5p results in a 17% rise in quantity demanded, which is less than the 50% fall in price. The PED = 0.34. As this is less than 1, the good is **inelastic**.

Factors that influence PED

1. **Number of close substitutes within the market** – The more close substitutes available in a market, the more elastic demand will be in response to a change in price. A large rise in the price of one brand of washing powder will result in many consumers switching to one of the other brands. As a result, demand will be **elastic**. A large rise in the price of petrol will only lead to a very small fall in demand as there are no close substitutes. As a result, demand will be **inelastic**.

2. **Luxuries and necessities – Necessities** tend to have a more **inelastic** demand curve, whereas **luxury goods** and services tend to be more **elastic**. If prices rise, most consumers will only marginally reduce their consumption of necessities, such as bread, but they are more likely to cut back on their purchases of luxuries that they do not actually need. For example, the demand for opera tickets is more elastic than the demand for urban rail travel. The demand for holiday air travel is more elastic than the demand for business air travel.

3. **Percentage of income spent on a good** – It may be the case that the smaller the proportion of income spent on a good or service, the more inelastic demand will be. A 10% rise in the price of a good costing a few pence, such as matches, is more likely to be absorbed than a 10% rise in the price of a good costing thousands of pounds. As a result, demand for more expensive items, which take up a large proportion of income, is likely to be more sensitive to price changes.

4. **Habit forming goods** – Goods such as cigarettes and drugs tend to be inelastic in demand. Preferences are such that habitual consumers of these products become de-sensitised to any price changes.

5. **Time period under consideration** – Demand tends to be **more elastic in the long run** rather than in the short run. This is because it takes time for consumers to adjust their spending habits following a change in price.

PED and pricing decisions

It is important for producers to know the PED of their output when making pricing decisions. Pricing decisions have a key impact on a firm's total revenue and profit.

● **Total revenue** = selling price x quantity sold.

● **Profit** = total revenue – total cost.

Price elasticity has a key impact on both variables.

● When a good is **price elastic** a **fall in price** will cause a **rise in total spending** on the good.

● When demand is **price inelastic** a **rise in price** will cause a **rise in total spending** on the good.

Figure 3.2

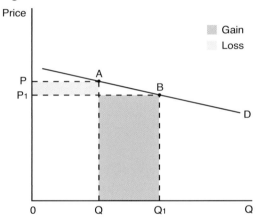

In Figure 3.2, demand is **price elastic**. At the original price P, total revenue was equal to the area OPAQ. Following the price fall to P_1, the new area of total revenue is equal to OP_1BQ_1. The fall in price from P to P_1 results in a rise in total revenue because **the area of gain exceeds the area of loss**.

Although there is a rise in total revenue it cannot be immediately assumed that a firm's profit will rise. This is because there is also a **rise in the firm's total costs** as output has increased from Q to Q_1. In this instance the **effect on profit is therefore ambiguous** as both revenue and costs have increased. It is impossible to tell accurately whether profits will rise or fall.

Figure 3.3

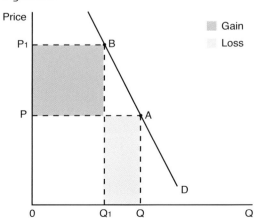

In Figure 3.3, demand is inelastic. At the original price P, total revenue was equal to the area OPAQ. Following the price rise to P_1, the new area of total revenue is equal to OP_1BQ_1. The rise in price from P to P_1 results in a rise in total revenue **because the area of gain exceeds the area of loss**.

The effect on profit in this case is more clear-cut because there is also a **fall in the firm's total costs** as output has decreased from Q to Q_1. As the firm's revenue has increased while its costs have fallen, its **profit will rise**.

Other uses of PED

If a firm knows the price elasticity of demand of its output it can use this information to calculate how much demand will vary following a change in price. Suppose the PED for baked beans is (-)0.4, it is possible to calculate exactly how much demand will fall following a rise in price.

The percentage change in demand = percentage change in price x PED.

If prices rose by 10%, then quantity demanded will fall by 4% (10% x -0.4) = -4%.

This information can be used by firms for **business planning**:

- to estimate changes in **production levels**.
- to identify whether **employment** in the firm will need to change.
- to analyse how changes in demand will affect **stocks**.

Income elasticity of demand (YED)

Income elasticity of demand measures the responsiveness of demand in percentage terms to a change in the **real incomes** of consumers.

$$\text{Income elasticity of demand (YED)} = \frac{\text{\% change in the quantity demanded of good X}}{\text{\% change in the real income of consumers}}$$

Normal and inferior goods

Normal goods are defined as those with a positive YED. Mobile phones, steak, air travel and foreign holidays are examples.

If the YED > 1, the good is considered to be a **luxury** and the proportion of income, or **budget share**, spent on the good rises with income. If the YED < 1, the good is considered to be a **necessity** and the **budget share falls** with income.

Inferior goods are defined as those with a **negative YED**. Examples may include bus journeys and own-label foods. When income rises, consumers may opt for superior alternatives in the form of private transport and branded food respectively.

Using income elasticity of demand

The value of an income elasticity is important to a firm as it determines the size of a **shift in demand**. Suppose a computer firm has two products, a desktop with an income elasticity of +0.5 and a laptop with an income elasticity of +3.5. If real national incomes are forecast to grow by 3% next year the firm can calculate the rise in demand for its products. Demand for desktops will rise by 1.5% (3% x +0.5 = 1.5%) and demand for laptops will increase by 10.5% (3% x +3.5 = 10.5%). The demand for laptops will shift further to the right than the demand for desktops.

The firm can use the YED estimate when **planning** changes in **output, employment and stocks**. When a product has a high income elasticity of demand, such as laptops, producers should be aware that demand will be highly sensitive to the living standards of consumers. In an **economic boom**, they can expect rising sales as demand shifts to the right but, in a **recession**, they should be prepared for falling demand and a fall in their **total revenue**.

The demand for **luxury boats** is likely to be more sensitive to the **economic cycle** than the demand for **basic foods** in supermarkets.

Cross-price elasticity of demand (XPED)

This is defined as the **responsiveness of demand for good X following changes in the price of a related good Y**.

Cross Price Elasticity of Demand (XPED) $= \dfrac{\text{\% change in the demand for good X}}{\text{\% change in the price of good Y}}$

- **XPED will be positive for substitute goods.** A rise in the price of local bus travel, which is a substitute for rail travel, should cause a rise in the demand for rail travel. When the substitutes are close substitutes, the value of XPED should be high.

- **XPED will be negative for complements.** A rise in the price of DVD players should cause a fall in demand not only for these products, but also for DVDs as the two goods are in joint demand. When the complements are closely related, the value of XPED should be high.

- **XPED will be zero** (or close to it) for completely unrelated goods.

Using cross price elasticity of demand

The firm can use a XPED estimate when **planning** changes in **output, employment and stocks** in response to changes in the price of substitutes or complements. When the product has a close substitute, such as a brand of washing powder, producers should be aware that demand will be highly sensitive to changes in the price of competing products. A rise in the price of a rival brand will cause a large outward shift in demand.

Price elasticity of supply (PES)

This is defined as the **responsiveness of quantity supplied to a change in the good's own price**.

$\text{PES} = \dfrac{\text{\% change in the quantity supplied of good X}}{\text{\% change in the price of good X}}$

Diagrams for different PES values

Figure 3.4(a)

Figure 3.4(b)

Figure 3.4(c)

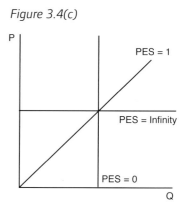

Figure 3.4 shows supply curves with different PES values. It is worth noting that any straight line supply curve that goes through the origin has unitary PES.

- **If the PES is greater than one, the good is elastic.** Supply is highly responsive to a change in price. A straight line supply curve that is elastic will cut the price axis (see Figure 3.4(a)). If the price rose from 10p to 11p, then the PES would be 4. The percentage change in quantity supplied is 40% while the percentage change in price is 10%.

- **If the PES is less than one, the good is inelastic.** Supply is not very responsive to changes in price. A straight line supply curve that is inelastic will cut the quantity axis (see Figure 3.4(b)). If the price fell from 10p to 5p, then the PES would be 0.7. The percentage change in quantity supplied is 35% while the percentage change in price is 50%.

- **If the PES is equal to 1, the good has unit elasticity.** The percentage change in quantity supplied is equal to the percentage change in price. Any straight line supply curve that originates from the origin has a PES of equal to one (see Figure 3.4(c)).

- **If the PES is equal to zero, the good is totally inelastic.** A change in price has no effect on the quantity supplied. The supply to the market is assumed to be fixed and will not change with price (see Figure 3.4(c)). A football stadium has a totally inelastic supply curve as the stadiums capacity cannot be changed even if there is massive demand from spectators to watch a match.

- **If the PES is infinity, the good is perfectly elastic.** Any change in price will see quantity supplied fall to zero (see Figure 3.4(c)).

Factors that influence PES

To understand whether supply is likely to be elastic, consider the following factors affecting whether firms can respond to price increases by expanding supply:

1. **Level of spare capacity** – if firms are working well below **full capacity** they can increase supply quickly and will have elastic supply curves. The higher the amount of spare capacity, the more elastic the supply. This is particularly relevant when an industry has experienced a downturn in demand leaving plenty of **under-utilised** productive resources.

2. **Substitutability of factors of production** – if factors of production can be easily moved into the production of a good or service, supply will be elastic. If resources used to make CD players were switched into the production of MP3 players, when demand for MP3 players increased then supply could have responded to meet the demand easily.

3. **Level of stocks and work in progress** – if firms have low levels of **stocks** (or **inventories**) they may not be able to respond quickly to changes in demand and will therefore have inelastic supply curves. In contrast, when a producer has a high level of unsold stocks they can supply extra output quickly to a market (although they may have to discount prices heavily to offload excess stock). This is sometimes seen in the car industry.

4. **Time period under consideration** – in the **short run**, at least one factor is assumed to be fixed. This will tend to limit the elasticity of supply. Supply will become more elastic in the **long run** when all factor inputs in the production process can be varied and a business can alter the scale of production to meet changing demand.

5. **Production lags** – in some industries there are clearly understood **production lags** where there is an inevitable time lag between using the factor inputs and the final product becoming available. This includes agricultural markets where supply cannot always respond elastically to fluctuations in demand. In the very short run the supply of products, such as cereals, may be perfectly inelastic.

Point elasticity of demand

Point elasticity of demand *(this section is required only for the OCR specification)*

The **price elasticity of demand varies along a straight line demand curve**. At the top of the demand curve, price is high and quantity demanded is low. A small percentage reduction in price gives a very large percentage increase in quantity because the change in quantity is high as a proportion of its original low value. Elasticity is thus very high at the top of the curve. By similar reasoning, it is very low at the bottom of the demand curve.

The basic formula for price elasticity of demand measures the elasticity between two different points on the demand curve. This is not ideal because:

- As a result of the fact that elasticity actually varies along the length of a demand curve, the basic formula gives inaccurate results when the two points are far apart on the demand curve.

● The formula gives different values depending on which of the two points is chosen as the original point for calculating the percentage changes in price and quantity.

Point elasticity of demand is more accurate because it calculates elasticity at a specific point on the demand curve. It is calculated as:

Price elasticity of demand (PED) =

$$\frac{\text{Price of good X}}{\text{Quantity demanded of good X}} \quad \text{x} \quad \frac{1}{\text{Gradient of demand curve for good X at that point}}$$

The gradient of a straight line demand curve is constant whichever point on that curve is chosen.

Using the point elasticity of demand formula we can see that the elasticity value of any demand curve is infinite at the point where it cuts the price axis. This is because the quantity of the good demanded is zero at this point and because there are an infinite number of zeros in any other number, the price of the good divided by the quantity demanded must be infinite. By similar reasoning, the elasticity is zero where the demand curve cuts the quantity axis. At the mid-point of a straight line demand curve, the price divided by the quantity demanded is equal to the gradient. The elasticity is thus unitary (PED = Gradient x 1/gradient = 1). The varying elasticity along a straight line demand curve is shown in Figure 3.5

Figure 3.5

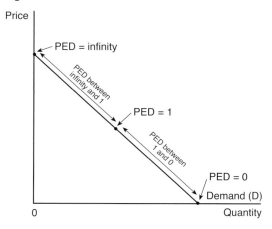

Point elasticity of supply

Point elasticity of supply (*this section is only required for the OCR specification*)

Point elasticity of supply is calculated as:

Price elasticity of supply (PES) =

$$\frac{\text{Price of good X}}{\text{Quantity supplied of good X}} \quad \text{x} \quad \frac{1}{\text{Gradient of supply curve for good X at that point}}$$

For any straight line supply curve which passes through the origin, the price divided by the quantity supplied is always equal to the gradient of the curve. This means that the PES is one (unitary) along the length of the entire curve. For any straight line supply curve cutting the price axis, price divided by the quantity supplied is always greater than the gradient. Hence, price elasticity of supply is greater than one (elastic) along the entire curve. Any straight line supply curve cutting the price axis has elasticity of less than one (inelastic). Supply curves of differing elasticities are shown in Figure 3.4.

Chapter

4

Paper 1: Introductory concepts → **Markets generally work well** → Sometimes markets fail → This may justify government intervention → Government failure sometimes occurs

Production, costs and revenue

The material in this chapter is primarily targeted on the needs of those students following the AQA and OCR AS-level specifications or anyone studying for a full A-level. It is anticipated that the material on specialisation and the division of labour in Chapter 1 will be sufficient for students taking the Edexcel A exam at AS-level.

The activity of firms

Firms combine **factors of production** (land, labour, capital and enterprise) into **output** (goods and services). The production of output results in costs for the firm, but the sale of output generates revenue. Costs relate to the supply side of a market, while revenue relates to demand.

Short run

This is the period of time in which at least one factor of production is **fixed** (usually capital). Labour is typically regarded as a **variable factor**.

It is impossible to put an actual length of time on the short run. A market trader may be able to buy a new stall and hire a new pitch in a day; a firm producing nuclear power could take a decade to build a new power station.

Long run

This is the period of time in which all factors are variable in quantity and it is possible for the firm to move to a new scale of production.

Costs of production

An economist measures the firm's production costs as the **opportunity cost** of the factors of production used (the revenue that the factor could have generated in its next best use).

Fixed costs

These are costs that do not vary with output. They must be paid in the short run even if no output is produced. Examples include the rent on premises, which must be paid until the existing contract expires.

Variable costs

These are costs that vary in proportion to the output. Examples might include electricity and gas costs.

Total costs

The total cost of production consists of the fixed costs plus variable costs: $TC = TFC + TVC$.

Average costs

Average fixed cost (AFC) is simply the total fixed cost (TFC) divided by quantity of output produced (Q): $AFC = TFC/Q$.

Average variable cost (AVC) is the total variable cost (TVC) divided by quantity: $AVC = TVC/Q$.

Average (total) cost (AC) is the total cost divided by the quantity produced: $AC = TC/Q$. Since TC consists of TFC and TVC, this is the same as $AC = (TFC + TVC)/Q$ or $AC = AFC + AVC$.

When output is graphed on the horizontal axis and costs on the vertical axis the average (total) cost curve is likely to be U-shaped. In the short run, increases in output are achieved by adding more of a variable factor such as labour to the production process. Average costs are likely to fall initially, as increased **division of labour** and hence **gains from specialisation** are possible, but later rise due to the effects of **diminishing returns to labour**.

Marginal cost	Marginal cost (MC) is the additional cost of making one extra unit of output and can be calculated as the change in total costs divided by the change in output.

Long run production and returns to scale	In the long run, all factors of production are variable. When a firm wishes to increase output it can increase all the factors of production (land labour and capital).

● **Increasing returns** to scale occur when the % change in output > % change in inputs.

● **Decreasing returns** to scale occur when the % change in output < % change in inputs.

● **Constant returns** to scale occur when the % change in output = % change in inputs.

Increasing returns to scale influence the long run average cost curve (see next section) by creating **economies of scale**; decreasing returns to scale are associated with diseconomies of scale. The **minimum efficient scale** describes the lowest quantity of output that the firm can produce while fully exploiting all available economies of scale. The expected shape of the long run average cost curve is shown in Figure 4.1.

Figure 4.1: The long run average cost curve

Internal economies of scale	Internal economies of scale result from the growth of the firm itself and lead to a movement along the long run average cost curve. They are usually categorised into technical economies, marketing economies, managerial economies, financial economies and risk-bearing economies.

Technical economies	These relate to the production and distribution process. Examples include:

● Larger firms can employ and combine specialist machinery that should reduce the average costs of production. For example, a large supermarket could install bar code technology reducing the average cost of recording and ordering stock. It would not, however, be economically viable for a small corner shop to buy this technology. Further, the cost of the capital is essentially fixed, and can be spread across increased output to achieve economies of scale.

● Within larger firms there is also greater scope for the **specialisation of labour**, reducing AC. The production line in many car plants is a good example of this concept.

● The **law of increased dimensions**. Doubling the height and width of a tanker or building can lead to a more than proportionate increase in the cubic capacity. Examples of industries where this is important include: food retailing, hotels, motor manufacturing, oil & gas distribution, airlines, transportation, warehousing/storage

Marketing economies	These relate to buying and selling. As a firm grows in size it can spread its advertising budget over a larger output, but most importantly it can purchase its factor inputs in bulk at negotiated discounted prices. A large firm may have **monopsony (buying) power**. Supermarkets have used their power to drive down the cost paid to suppliers, e.g. UK farmers.

Managerial economies	These arise as a result of the application of the **division of labour** to management. For example, larger supermarkets can afford to employ specialist buyers who can reduce their buying costs. Better management and the use of specialist equipment, such as networked computers that improve communication, raise productivity and reduce average costs.
Financial economies	Larger firms normally have greater access to credit facilities, with favourable rates of borrowing in comparison to smaller firms.
Risk-bearing economies	As firms grow, they may be able to reduce costs by effectively self-insuring. For example, product diversification reduces the risk associated with the failure of any one product because the firm can be sustained by more successful lines of output.
External economies of scale	External economies of scale arise from the growth in the size of the industry as a whole. Firms within the industry will experience a fall in long run average costs, particularly if the firms are clustered in one geographical region. The firm's entire long run average cost curve shifts downwards as the industry grows. One example of an external economy of scale is that component suppliers for the industry may start to set up in business, able to produce parts at a cheaper cost than if individual firms tried to make them.
Diseconomies of scale	Diseconomies of scale arise when the firm grows beyond the scale of production that minimises average cost. Examples include: ● **Control** – monitoring how productive each worker is in a modern corporation is both imperfect and costly. ● **Co-ordination** – it is difficult to co-ordinate complicated production processes and they may break down. Achieving efficient flows of information in large businesses is expensive. ● **Co-operation** – workers in large firms may feel a sense of alienation. If they do not consider themselves to be an integral part of the business their productivity may fall.
Revenue	Revenue is the income generated from the sale of a good or service. The revenue earned by a firm depends on the willingness of consumers to buy the product at any given price and therefore relates to demand.
Total revenue	The total revenue earned from sales of a product can be measured by its price multiplied by quantity sold: $TR = P \times Q$. This can be illustrated as the area under the demand curve (see the section on PED and pricing decision in Chapter 3).
Marginal revenue	Marginal revenue (MR) is the addition to revenue from selling one extra unit of the good or service.
Average revenue	Average revenue (AR) is the total revenue divided by quantity sold: $AR = TR/Q$. Since $TR = P \times Q$, we can also state average revenue as $AR = (P \times Q)/Q$, which reduces to $AR = P$. The average revenue from the sale of each unit of a product is simply the price for which that product sells. Because the demand curves tells us the price at which any given quantity can be sold, it also tells us the average revenue for that quantity and so the demand curve and the average revenue curve are one and the same thing.

Revenue curves

In Figure 4.2 the demand curve (AR curve) facing the firm is perfectly elastic. As the firm sells each additional unit at a constant price, AR must equal MR. The total revenue curve is a straight line because marginal revenue is both positive and constant. This situation applies to firms that are **price-takers**, operating in highly competitive markets (see Chapter 5).

In Figure 4.3, the firm faces a downward sloping demand curve. This situation applies to a firm with some degree of monopoly (**price-making**) power (see Chapter 5). To sell an extra unit of the good, the firm must reduce the price, including the units that it would have sold at the existing price. This means that marginal revenue from the sale of the extra unit is less than the price (which is equal to average revenue) for which it is sold. Thus the MR curve lies below the MR curve.

It can be mathematically proven that the MR curve is always twice as steep the AR curve. Total revenue is maximised when MR is zero and the elasticity of demand is equal to 1. This is the exact mid-point of a straight line demand curve extending from one axis to the other (mathematically, elasticity is infinity where the demand curve touches the vertical axis and zero where it cuts the horizontal axis – see Chapter 1 for an explanation). Up to point A, MR is positive so any increases in output result in a rise in total revenue. Beyond this point MR is negative and any rise in output causes a fall in total revenue.

Figure 4.2

Figure 4.3

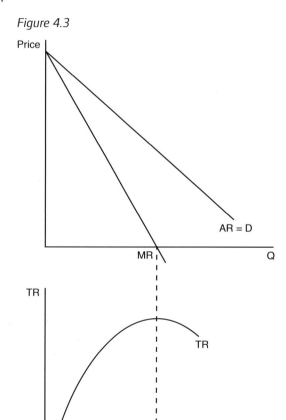

Profit

Profit is the reward to enterprise as a factor of production. It can be calculated as the gap between total revenue and total cost:

Profit = Total revenue − Total cost

Competitive and concentrated markets

This chapter is primarily targeted on the needs of students following the AS level specification of AQA. This material is not directly required for the Edexcel A and OCR specifications at AS-level. A more in-depth treatment of this material is required by all exam boards at A-level, however, typically taught in Year 2 of the course.

A market is **competitive** when there are lots of small firms with similar market shares and no firm has significant power over the market. By contrast, a market is **concentrated** if a small number of firms hold a large market share. The **concentration ratio** measures the combined market share of the largest 'x' firms in the market

In the fictional market for widgets shown below, the 3-firm concentration ratio is 81% and the 4-firm concentration ratio is 90%. The market for widgets could appropriately be described as concentrated, although it should be noted that there is no specific threshold for a market to be labelled as concentrated.

Market share for widgets (percentages)

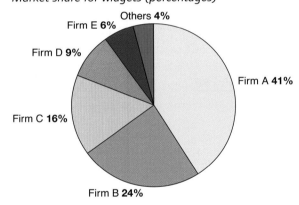

Market structures

The degree of market concentration is perhaps the chief characteristic which helps to define a **market structure**. The list of such characteristics include:

● **The degree of market concentration.**

● **The degree of product differentiation.** The products of different firms within the same market are **substitutes** for one another. When these products are perfect substitutes for one another they are known as **homogenous**. However, products can also be differentiated in terms of either their physical characteristics or through branding and image characteristics.

● **The information held by market participants.** Consumers and firms may hold some knowledge of the various products in the market and their prices but this knowledge is not necessarily perfect.

● **The ease of market entry and exit.** Some markets are less costly for firms to enter and leave than others, so the height of **barriers to entry** and exit vary from one market to another.

The structure of a market influences the behaviour or **conduct** of the firms within it. This in turn affects the outcome or **performance** of the market, leading economists to refer to the **structure-conduct-performance** model of the theory of the firm.

Thus we expect the behaviour of firms in a perfectly competitive market to be different from those operating in a monopoly. As a result of these behaviours, economists usually predict that a competitive market will perform more efficiently than a monopoly.

Perfect competition and monopoly represent opposite ends of the **spectrum of market structures** shown below. In between are various form of **imperfect competition** such as **monopolistic competition** and **oligopoly** which are studied in detail in A-level Year 2.

0%	Increasing Market Concentration		100%
Perfect Competition	Monopolistic Competition	Oligopoly	Monopoly

Perfect competition

Perfectly competitive markets have the following **characteristics**:

1. Many buyers and many sellers (0% concentration).

2. Homogeneous products (each firm's product is identical).

3. Perfect information (each firm and consumer has perfect knowledge of market conditions, such as the price charged by each firm in the market).

4. There are no entry or exit barriers (so there is complete freedom of entry and exit to and from the market).

We expect to see the following conduct in a perfectly competitive market:

● Firms behave as **price-takers**. They have no control over the price of their products and must accept the price determined by the **market forces** of supply and demand. If a firm attempted to charge even a fraction of one penny more than its rivals, demand for its product would in theory fall to zero. This is because rational consumers would switch to the perfect substitutes which they know are offered by other firms in the market. Thus the firm faces a perfectly elastic demand curve, which is also its average revenue curve (see Chapter 4 to understand why).

● Consumers are also price-takers. There is no **monopsony** power – in other words no consumer buys enough of the market output to have the power to lower prices.

● There is no branding or non-price competition of any kind.

Firms in competitive markets typically make lower profits than firms in more concentrated markets. This is because competition puts downwards pressure on prices.

The **functions of the price mechanism** (see Chapter 6) are based on the assumption that firms are price-takers, responding to the price-signals of the market. Indeed, the supply curve shows the quantities of a good that firms are willing and able to supply at different market prices over a given time period. Thus, supply curves only exist in competitive markets. The claim that **markets generally work well** is made on the basis that competitive markets deliver a **performance** in which **productive efficiency** and **allocative efficiency** are both achieved.

Although perfect competition may not exist in the real world, there are still markets that can be considered to be highly competitive. Good examples of competitive markets include: Book retailing, clothing, computer hardware, home and car insurance, opticians, parcel delivery.

Monopoly

The market **structure** of **pure monopoly** exists when there is a single supplier in a market, typically protected by high **barriers to entry**. Some pure monopolies do exist, even though such markets are rare. Even powerful firms such as Apple do not enjoy a market share of 100%!

Monopoly power

Monopoly power can be taken as the ability of the firm to influence its own price, rather than having it dictated by market forces. Firms operating in other types of **concentrated** markets besides pure monopolies often derive monopoly power from their high **market shares** and may also enjoy protection from **high**

barriers to entry. When firms are able to **differentiate** their product from substitutes produced by other firms, this creates a basis for consumer loyalty, allowing firms to raise their prices while retaining some or all of their customers. **Consumer inertia** may also confer monopoly power. Gas suppliers, for example, may be able to retain customers after putting up their prices because of the effort involved for the consumer if he wishes to switch providers.

How do monopolies develop?

Monopolies can develop in the following ways:

● **Horizontal integration**

Where two firms join at the same stage of production in the same industry. For example two car manufacturers merge, or a leading bank successfully takes over another bank.

● **Vertical integration**

Where a firm develops market power by integrating with the different stages of production in an industry e.g. by buying its suppliers or controlling the main retail outlets. A good example is the oil industry where many of the leading companies are both producers and refiners of crude oil.

● **Creation of a statutory monopoly**

Some key industries are given monopoly status. For example, water companies such as Severn Trent have a legally protected monopoly on supply of domestic water and sewerage services.

● **Franchises and Licences**

These give a firm the right to operate in a market – and are usually open to renewal every few years. Examples include:

  ● Commercial radio licences

  ● Commercial television

  ● Local taxi route licences

  ● Regional rail services

  ● The National Lottery

● **Internal expansion of a firm**

Firms can generate higher sales and increase market share by expanding their operations and exploiting possible economies of scale.

Monopolies and market failure

Where a single firm supplies the whole market, it is not subject to the competitive pressure of market forces. It can therefore set its own price, leading to a break-down of the price mechanism. Economists predict that the **conduct** of a monopoly firm will be to raise prices and restrict quantity of output (see the next sub-section and Figure 5.1 for an explanation of why this restriction of quantity is necessary). The implication for the **performance** of the market is that fewer resources are allocated to this line of production than would have been the case if the price mechanism had directed resource allocation. These resources are now allocated to another use where they will not produce as much **utility**. Hence monopoly creates an inefficient resource allocation and is a source of **market failure**.

The monopolist is constrained by the demand curve

In the absence of government intervention, the only constraint on the ability of a monopoly to set its own price is the market demand curve, which shows the various price and quantity combinations that the market will support.

If the monopoly firm wishes to raise price above the level that would have prevailed in a competitive market, he must accept that demand will contract. Figure 5.1 shows this. The monopolist raises price from the competitive level of Pc to Pm. Demand contracts from Qc to Qm. There is not enough demand at price Pm to allow the monopolist to choose point X.

The damage caused by monopoly

Figure 5.1

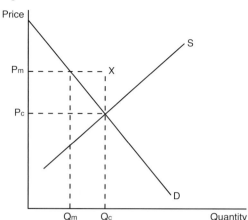

The above analysis demonstrates that to use his price-making power to raise prices, the monopolist must accept that demand will contract (in other words, the monopolist must restrict supply to raise price). It is thus often said that monopolies are guilty of **exploiting consumers**.

The following analysis is not explicitly required by any of the exam boards at AS-level but can be very useful.

Figure 5.2

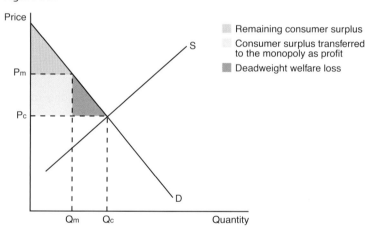

By raising price and restricting quantity, the monopoly reduces the level of consumer surplus compared to a competitive market. Some of the consumer surplus on the Qm units that are still sold (see Figure 5.2) is transferred to the monopoly firm as higher profit. The surplus that consumers previously enjoyed on the (Qc –Qm) units is lost, however. This is known as a **deadweight welfare loss** and is a measure of the damage caused by the inefficient resource allocation brought about by the monopoly.

Can monopoly or monopoly power be beneficial?

Possible benefits of monopoly include:

1. **Competitive processes** occur even in markets which are concentrated. Many large firms compete vigorously with one another rather than exploiting the consumer. This can lead to various benefits, such as:

    ● Large firms may strive to improve products and the quality of service in order to gain an edge over rivals. One facet of this is that profits may be reinvested into research and development, leading to innovation (enhancing the **dynamic efficiency** of the economy). Even pure monopolies might act in this way in order to increase the entry barriers to their market, although lack of competitive pressure may make this unnecessary. Pure monopolies may also avoid wasteful duplication of research.

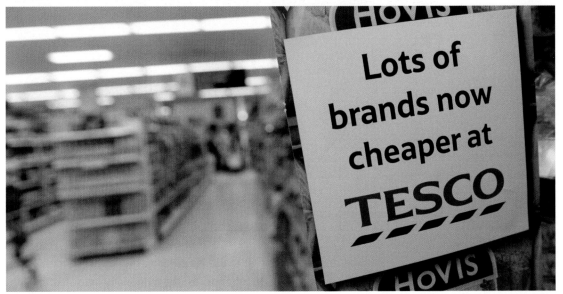

Firms such as Tesco sustain their power by selling high volumes of goods at low prices.

- The branding that firms use to win and protect market share can act as a guarantee of quality to the consumer.

- Some large firms in the real world sustain their power by selling high volumes of goods at low prices. Tesco and ToysRus are examples. This may actually increase consumer surplus.

- Advertising expenditure undertaken in the pursuit of monopoly power may help to fund television channels, newspapers, sports and community events and so on.

2. Monopolies may lower costs of production by exploiting economies of scale that are not available to smaller firms. This could be shown as a movement along the long-run average cost curve (see Chapter 4).

3. Some monopolies are particularly useful to consumers in virtue of the sheer numbers of people using the firm's products. This is particularly true in the case of hi-tech markets. Microsoft's near monopoly over office software means that workers can move from firm to firm without needing retraining, for example. In a similar way, it suits customers that e-Bay has a near monopoly over online auctions because sellers are guaranteed to reach a large market and buyers have many products to choose from. Each new user of social media sites such as Facebook and Twitter increases the value of the sites to other users. Thus there are **compatibility benefits** from all participants using the same technology in some markets.

Objective of firms

Profit is an important objective of most firms. The traditional (**neoclassical**) approach to analysing competitive and concentrated markets outlined in this chapter assumes that firms aim to maximise profits. This is the reason, for example, that monopolists are predicted to raise prices and restrict output.

Profit maximising may seem a reasonable assumption, but we should remember it is only an assumption. Firms do sometimes pursue other objectives, including survival, growth and increasing market share. If firms pursue alternative objectives to profit maximisation, this will affect their conduct. If a firm is trying to increase its market share, for example, is may reduce its price in order to try to sell more output.

Alternative objectives are particularly likely if those in charge of running the firm are not those who own the firm and who directly benefit from its profits (this is known as the **divorce of ownership and control**). This situation may well arise in limited companies where the owners (shareholders) may lack effective mechanisms to control the behaviour of directors and management.

Chapter

6

Paper 1: Introductory concepts → **Markets generally work well** → Sometimes markets fail → This may justify government intervention → Government failure sometimes occurs

The price mechanism

Competitive markets

A competitive market is one in which no individual supplier or consumer can influence the price. Instead, the price is set by the interaction of overall market supply and demand, to which consumers and firms respond. If there is an excess demand or supply at the current market price, this creates an incentive for participants in the market to change their behaviour. Thus **market forces** push the price towards an **equilibrium**, market clearing, level (as outlined in Chapter 2).

Allocative efficiency

Remember that the subject of Economics is concerned with the study of the allocation of scarce resources. An efficient resource allocation occurs when society's scarce resources are allocated between competing uses in such a way as the total **utility or satisfaction** derived from the resources is maximised.

The price mechanism and its functions

The price mechanism is the system by which changes in the relative prices of goods serve to allocate resources in a market economy. This occurs through the three functions of the price mechanism. Suppose that, with the market for a good initially in equilibrium, demand for the good then increases. The three functions would work in the following way:

Rationing function – In the first instance, the increase in demand for the good creates an excess demand for the product at the current price. Market forces will then cause the price to start rising; this rations the available supply of the product and those consumers willing to pay higher prices for it are those who purchase the good.

Signalling function – The rising price acts as a signal to producers that there is an excess demand for the product.

Incentive function – Because the higher price raises the profit margin on each unit of the good supplied, it creates an incentive for producers to expand supply. Resources are reallocated from other lines of production in order to expand supply of the product which has experienced a rise in demand.

In our example, the **price mechanism** has directed resources in line with consumer demand. This is sometimes known as **consumer sovereignty**. Demand comes from consumers who are assumed to be attempting to maximise their own utility. Thus the price mechanism has acted as an '**invisible hand**' (as described by Adam Smith) allocating resources in such a way to maximise utility or satisfaction.

The price mechanism can also achieve an efficient allocation of resources following a change in supply. If, for example, higher production costs led to a decrease of supply, there would again be an excess demand. This would result in a higher price and the **rationing function** would work as described above. However, this time the **signal** is received by the consumer who has an **incentive** to switch to substitute goods which are now relatively cheaper. There is therefore a contraction of demand. Less of the good is traded and resources are released to other uses.

Conditions for the price mechanism to achieve an efficient resource allocation

For the price mechanism to allocate resources efficiently, as outlined in the previous sub-section, a number of conditions must hold:

- Market participants must not be able to influence the price. This implies a **lack of monopoly power** on the part of suppliers. On the demand side, the equivalent concept is the absence of **monopsony** buying power.

- Market participants adopt **maximising behaviour** as outlined in Chapter 1. For example, consumers are selfish (acting to maximise their own utility or satisfaction) and **rational** (not making mistakes in maximising utility or satisfaction); firms act to maximise profits.

● There are no **externalities** (see Chapter 7) associated with the production or consumption of the product.

● **Perfect information** is available to all market participants. For example, consumers know about all the alternatives available for them when they spend their limited income.

● **Resources are perfectly mobile** between competing uses, so that they can be reallocated to other products when market forces cause changes in the relative prices of goods.

If these conditions are not satisfied, it is likely that **market failure** will result. It is also worth noting that an **efficient** resource allocation in no way implies that the outcome is **fair (equitable)**. A lack of equity is another possible source of market failure, although this concept is controversial because it is **normative** in nature.

Consumer surplus

The price that a consumer is willing to pay for a good reflects the utility or satisfaction that he or she derives from it. In competitive markets, there is a single market price paid by all consumers. Those who would have been willing to pay more than this price receive a surplus.

Consumer surplus is the difference between what consumers are **willing** to pay for a good or service (indicated by the position of the demand curve) and what they **actually pay** (the market price).

Consumer surplus is shown in Figure 6.1 below.

Figure 6.1

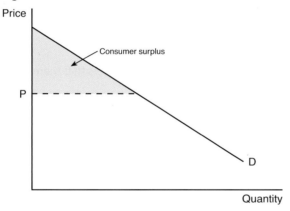

Changes in demand and consumer surplus

When there is a shift in the demand curve leading to a change in the equilibrium price and quantity traded, the amount of consumer surplus will alter.

This is shown in Figure 6.2. Following a shift in demand from D to D_1, the price rises to P_1 and quantity traded expands to Q_1. Consumer surplus was initially shown by the triangle AP_0B. This rises to area EP_1C.

Figure 6.2

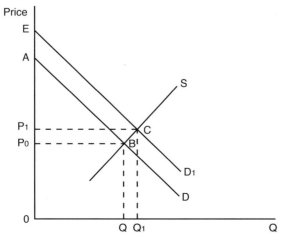

Producer surplus

Producer surplus is defined as the difference between what producers are willing and able to supply a good for (indicated by the position of the supply curve) and the price they actually receive.

Producer surplus is illustrated in Figure 6.3.

Figure 6.3

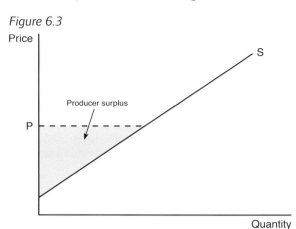

Relationships between goods

Sometimes two or more goods have special relationships in the price mechanism, so that a change in the market for one of the goods affects the market for another:

Substitutes – These are goods that are in **competitive demand** with one another, such as butter and margarine. A fall in the supply of butter will cause its price to rise and demand for it to contract. This serves to increase the demand for margarine (that is, to shift the demand curve to the right).

Complements – These are goods in **joint demand** such as dishwashers and dishwasher tablets. A fall in the supply of dishwashers would cause their price to rise and demand for them to contract. The demand for dishwasher tablets would then fall (shift to the left).

Joint supply – Some goods are by-products of other production processes. For example, bee keepers who produce honey are also able to supply beeswax for use on surfboards. An increase in the demand for honey causes its price to rise, leading to an extension of supply. This causes the supply of beeswax to increase (shift to the right).

Derived demand – The demand for some products is derived from the demand for others. For example, steel is rarely demanded for its own sake but for other uses such as construction. So the demand for steel is partly derived from the demand for buildings. When the supply of buildings increases, their price falls and demand expands. This then increases the demand for steel (demand shifts to the right). A common example of derived demand is that of labour, the demand for which is derived from the demand for the products and services that the workers produce.

Composite demand – Some goods are demanded for more than one purpose. Steel is needed not just for building but for making cars, for example. Its demand is composed of demand for these two uses and many others besides. If there is an increase in demand for steel for use in construction, this may reduce the supply of steel available to the car industry.

Composite supply – Some goods or services are supplied from more than one source. The supply of electricity, for example, is composed of electricity generated from fossil fuels, nuclear power and various renewable resources such as wind and solar power. These various sources are in competition with one another and, *ceteris paribus*, economists would predict that the cheapest source of electricity supply would be used. However, the various sources combine to satisfy our need for electricity

Applying the price mechanism to different markets

AQA, Edexcel and OCR all require that students can apply their understanding of demand and supply analysis and the price mechanism to real-world markets. The Edexcel AS-level specification states that this should include "local, national and global markets" while the OCR specification flags up commodity, housing and transport markets. The AQA specification does not highlight any markets in particular. Students of all specifications would be well advised to read the sections on unstable commodity prices in Chapter 8, even though the bulk of that chapter is only required for AS-level by AQA.

Market failure

The main causes of market failure are: 1. Imperfect information; 2. Externalities (including those associated with merit and demerit goods); 3. Public goods; 4. Monopoly power; 5. Resource immobility; 6. Unstable prices in commodity markets. The final source of market failure is different from the others because it is normative in nature: 7. An unfair distribution of income (lack of equity).

The OCR and Edexcel AS-level specifications only require coverage of the first three of these sources of market failure and therefore you may need only to study this chapter. Those taking the AQA AS-level exam and all students of other boards progressing to A-level Year 2 should be familiar with Chapter 8 too.

Imperfect information

Chapter 6 showed that the price mechanism will only allocate resources efficiently if market participants enjoy perfect information.

The price mechanism allows resources to follow consumer demand, but the result only maximises utility (satisfaction) on the assumption that consumers are rational, self-interested utility maximisers and that they have the correct information on which to base their decisions.

Suppose a consumer is choosing a flat screen television with a budget of £600. There are huge numbers of different products available. It is unlikely that a consumer will choose the one that maximises their utility unless they have information on a wide range of different televisions. The consumer would need to research information on the features of each television. These might include screen size, picture sharpness, connectivity to other devices, range of viewing angles and many others besides.

Similarly, firms must have full information, for example about the profit margins available to them in other lines of production. If this is not the case, firms cannot respond appropriately to the signals and incentives provided by the price mechanism.

Symmetric information refers to a situation where the buyer and seller of the product have the same information.

Asymmetric information occurs when either the buyer or seller possess more information than the other party.

Asymmetric information is a particular example of the problem of imperfect information. George Akerlof brought the issue to prominence when writing about the *Market for Lemons*, a lemon being a low quality second hand car, while a high quality car is a peach. The seller of a second hand car is likely to know whether it is a lemon or a peach, the buyer, however, has no way of telling. This could lead to a buyer mistakenly paying an excessive price for a lemon. Moreover, given the uncertainty, he/she is likely to be unwilling to pay the appropriate price for a high quality car (peach). This means that sellers are unlikely to bring peaches to market, because they will not be paid full value for them: it would seem that there cannot be an efficient market in high quality used cars!

Of course, there are ways in which sellers can attempt to **signal** the high quality of their 'peach', for example by maintaining a full service history. Buyers can protect themselves by paying for a mechanic to inspect the car before they buy. However, these practices themselves are an additional cost to those concerned arising from the **asymmetric information problem**.

Examples of asymmetric information are widespread. They include:

● Mechanics possessing specialist information about service and maintenance of cars, but this information is not known by the customer.

● Employers attempting to judge the quality of job applicants through an application form, references and a short interview. However, the applicant is likely to be better informed about his skills and personality than the firm that is considering hiring him.

● Sellers of houses covering up problems such as damp, cracks in walls and stains in carpets to hide them from prospective buyers.

● Those purchasing goods on e-Bay without actually seeing them, whereas the seller has a more complete knowledge of the product they are selling.

Moral hazard

Moral hazard occurs when one person takes more risks because they know that someone else bears the burden of those risks. Motorists may drive less carefully, for example, because insurance companies pay for any damage to their car. This is also an example of asymmetric information because the driver is more likely to know whether insurance cover will cause them to drive less carefully than the insurance company.

Moral hazard can be a source of market failure. For instance, if insured drivers are encouraged to take more risks, insurance firms will have to make more pay-outs and their costs will rise. This may raise the price of insurance and lead to a contraction of demand for it. The amount of insurance cover taken out may then be reduced to lower than the socially optimal level.

There are also equity issues in insurance: Those who drive less carefully as a result of being covered raise insurance premiums for all drivers, even those who drive carefully. If insurance firms could observe the behaviour of drivers, the problems of moral hazard would not exist. This is because each drive could be charged a premium which reflects the riskiness of their own driving. They would then have an incentive to drive carefully. This explains why some insurance companies have started issuing drivers with 'black boxes' or mobile phone apps which monitor their driving.

Motorists may drive less carefully because insurance companies pay for any damage to their car.

Other applications of moral hazard include the argument that banks and other financial institutions know they are too-big-to-fail. They may take more risks in an attempt to increase profits because they believe that government will step in and bail them out in the event that they make big losses and the future of the company is threatened.

Externalities

Externalities are defined as **third party** (or spillover) effects arising from the production or consumption of goods and services for which **no appropriate compensation** is paid (in other words, the effects are outside of the market). There are four main types of externality:

Positive externalities in consumption

Some goods carry third party benefits when they are consumed. Individuals who pay for health care are likely to be more productive workers thus generating third-party benefits for their employer, for instance. Equally, those who are immunised against contagious diseases create benefits for others because such diseases are less likely to be spread in society.

Negative externalities in consumption

The consumption of some goods and services is damaging to third parties. The effects of smoking cigarettes, for example, are not confined to the smoker but include third party effects such as passive smoking which may impact the health of others.

Positive externalities in production

Some production processes are helpful to third parties. The production of honey, for example, involves beekeeping. Bees pollinate plants which help to feed many other animals in the food chain. Anyone who gains from this is a third party beneficiary.

Negative externalities in production

Some production processes impose costs on third parties. The pollution emitted in industrial processes is an example. In the absence of government intervention, firms do not have to pay to pump waste into the environment. However, the pollution leads to poor air quality which damages third parties, especially those with respiratory illnesses such as asthma.

To distinguish between externalities in production and consumption, think about whether the effect on third parties would exist if the good were produced but never consumed. Emissions from factories are directly associated with the production of the goods and occur even if no one ever uses the goods which were made. However, the damage from cigarettes occurs largely when they are smoked rather than when they are made. The third party effects of smoking are therefore negative externalities in consumption.

Externalities cause **market failure** because they occur outside of the market. Individuals who generate positive externalities have no way of using the market to charge for doing so. Third parties who suffer from negative externalities have no way of using the market to gain compensation. Externalities are therefore a failure associated with **missing markets** because externalities are not traded. Goods associated with positive externalities are **under-consumer** and **under-provided** in the market system, while goods associated with negative externalities are **over-consumer** and **over-provided**.

Social costs and benefits

The full social cost or social benefit of an activity takes account of the effects of the activity on third parties:

Social cost = Private cost + External cost

Social benefit = Private benefit + External benefit

It is clear that externalities create a divergence between private and social costs and between private and social benefits. Because market transactions only reflect private costs and benefits, markets will fail to produce an optimal resource allocation from society's perspective when externalities are present.

Example: Private and external costs and benefits of car ownership

Private costs

- Road taxes
- Insurance
- Running costs: maintenance;
  fuel and depreciation

Private Benefits

- Satisfaction of running a privately owned car
- Increased mobility and flexibility of lifestyle
- Convenience

External costs of car ownership

- Traffic congestion reduces average speeds and lengthens journey times.

- Slower journeys increase transportation costs for goods and services and add to the overall cost of living in the economy. This makes domestic firms less competitive.

- High accident rates in areas with congested traffic impose extra costs on the National Health Service. Another major problem is air pollution, which causes asthma and heart attacks.

External benefits of car ownership

- Output of the motor car industry generates employment and income in the economy.

- The motor car industry creates hundreds of thousands of jobs in related **complementary industries**:
  · Vehicle insurance
  · Repair and maintenance
  · Petrol Retailing
  · Design industries

- High levels of tax on petrol bring in very large amounts of tax revenue for the Treasury each year.

Merit goods

Merit goods are defined as goods that are **under provided** in a market economy. The price mechanism allocates fewer resources to their production than is thought socially desirable.

The best known examples of merit goods are education and healthcare, which would be very substantially under provided in a pure free market economy because the **social benefits are greater than the private benefits**.

There are a number of reasons why education would be under provided in a free market economy:

- The external benefits of education would not be taken into account by individuals deciding whether to pay for schooling. The **social benefit of education exceeds the private benefit**.

- Individuals might underestimate the private benefits of education (for example, the benefit of higher earnings potential). This is an example of **imperfect information** affecting the ability of the price mechanism to allocate resources efficiently.

- Even if individuals judge the private benefits correctly, they might **discount** them (place less weight on them) because the benefits occur largely in the future, rather than when the education is paid for.

- Those paying for education are rarely the direct recipient of its benefits. Education would usually be paid for by parents rather than by students.

All these factors may serve to reduce demand below the levels that are socially desirable. In the end, because social costs and benefits are not easy to measure, the judgement that a good is a merit good becomes a matter of opinion (a value judgement), introducing a normative element to the analysis.

Demerit goods

Demerit goods are defined as goods that are **over provided** in the market economy. The price mechanism allocates more resources to their production than is thought socially desirable.

Examples of demerit goods include cigarettes, alcohol and drugs.

Consumption of these goods generates negative externalities, so that the **social cost of consumption exceeds the private costs**. Of course, these negative externalities are not accounted for by the price mechanism.

Just as with merit goods, there are problems of imperfect information associated with demerit goods. There is a danger of smoking leading to lung cancer, for example, but no individual knows whether he/she will get lung cancer until it happens. Individuals may underestimate the risk and place little weight on it because of the fact that if it happens at all it is likely to occur some way in the future. Individuals tend to underestimate the private costs of consuming demerit goods.

Marginal analysis of externalities

Marginal means 'one extra' or 'a little extra', thus the marginal benefit from a good is the benefit gained from one extra unit of consumption. Marginal concepts are important to economists, but they tend not to be examined at AS Level, being reserved instead for A-level Year 2. However, the Edexcel and OCR AS-level specifications do require students to be familiar with marginal analysis in relation to externalities.

The starting point here is to understand that:

● **Marginal private benefit** (**MPB**) is the benefit to the individual of consuming the last unit of a good. This is effectively the demand curve for a good.

● **Marginal private cost** (**MPC**) is the cost to a firm of producing the last unit of a good. This is effectively the supply curve for a good.

● **Marginal social benefit** (**MSB**) is the benefit to the individual consuming the good, plus the external benefit, of the last unit of the good.

● **Marginal social cost** (**MSC**) is the cost to the firm, plus the external cost, of producing the last unit of a good.

The **allocatively efficient** level of output in a market, known as the **social optimum** is achieved at the point where the marginal social benefit of the good is equal to the marginal social cost (**MSB = MSC**). This is because if MSB is greater than MSC, the consumption of an extra unit of the good will offer more benefit to society than it adds to society's costs. Production and consumption should therefore be expanded. By similar reasoning, if MSC is greater than MSB, production and consumption should be cut.

Diagrammatic analysis of externalities

Each exam board has slightly different requirements for the diagrams AS-level students will use to illustrate externalities. The diagrams needed for each of the largest three exam boards are shown in Figure 7.1 so that you can study those which are relevant to your course. Whether it is the demand or supply curve that shifts, the size of the externality is represented by the vertical distance between the original curve and the new one.

The triangular welfare loss areas included in the diagrams for Edexcel and OCR are found by the gap between marginal social benefit and marginal social cost between Q (the market outcome) and Q* (the best outcome for society, known as the social optimum). Q* also represents an **allocatively efficient** outcome. At Q* the condition MSB = MSC is satisfied (see previous section).

Figure 7.1 for AQA: Knowledge of four different diagrams is required, based on simple supply and demand analysis as shown.

Positive externalities in consumption (*this diagram can be used to illustrate merit goods*)

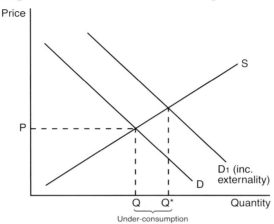

Under-consumption

Negative externalities in consumption (*this diagram can be used to illustrate demerit goods*)

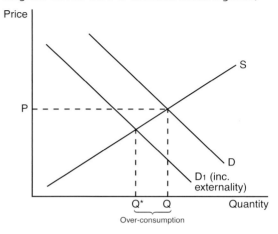

Over-consumption

Positive externalities in production

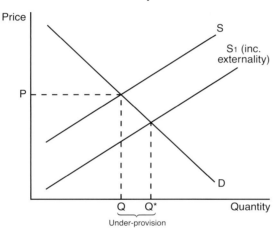

Under-provision

Negative externalities in production

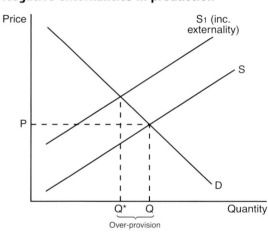

Over-provision

Figure 7.1 for Edexcel: Knowledge of two different diagrams is required, based on marginal analysis. Diagrams are required only for two of the four types of externalities: positive externalities in consumption and negative externalities in production. Students are expected to be able to identify the areas of welfare gain or loss as shown.

Positive externalities in consumption

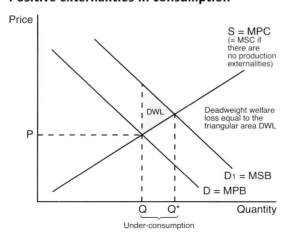

Under-consumption

Negative externalities in production

Over-provision

Figure 7.1 for OCR: Knowledge of four different diagrams is required, based on marginal analysis. There is no explicit expectation that students can identify the areas of welfare gain or loss on diagrams. However, they are included here as students may still find the concept of welfare gain or loss useful to employ in their answers.

Positive externalities in consumption

Negative externalities in consumption

Positive externalities in production

Negative externalities in production

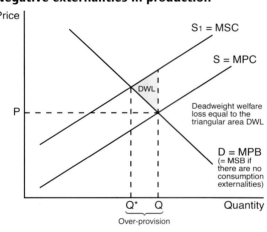

Public goods

Public goods are defined in terms of two key characteristics:

● **Non-excludability** – consumption of the good cannot be confined to those who have paid for it.

● **Non-rivalry in consumption** – the consumption by one individual does not reduce the availability of goods to others.

Many public goods possess a third characteristic:

● **Non-rejectability** – the consumer has no choice but to consume the good.

Examples of public goods include flood control systems, street lighting and national defence. A flood control system, such as the Thames Barrier, cannot be confined to those who have paid for the service. Also the consumption of the service by one household will not reduce its availability to others.

Most goods are **private goods**, which are excludable (you only get the good if you pay for it).

No consumer would pay for a public good that could be consumed for free if another household decided to purchase it. This is the **free-rider problem**. As a result, no public goods would be provided if it were left to the private sector. This is why governments intervene to ensure that resources are allocated to the production of public goods.

Public goods include flood control systems such as the Thames Barrier.

Note that this market failure is slightly different in one respect from many of the others. The market for public goods may be **missing** from the price mechanism, because public goods might not be provided by the private sector at all. This in contrast to other goods where the market is present but fails to achieve an efficient allocation of resources.

Quasi-public goods are products that are public in nature, but do not exhibit fully the features of non-excludability and non-rivalry. The road network in the UK is currently available to all, but could be made excludable via a system of tolls. There is also non-rivalry in consumption, but only up to an extent. Once the road becomes congested there is rivalry in consumption.

Chapter

8

Paper 1: Introductory concepts → Markets generally work well → **Sometimes markets fail** → This may justify government intervention → Government failure sometimes occurs

Market failure – monopoly, resource immobility, unstable commodity prices, lack of equity

Market failure

The main causes of market failure are: 1. Imperfect information; 2. Externalities (including those associated with merit and demerit goods); 3. Public goods; 4. Monopoly power; 5. Resource immobility; 6. Unstable prices in commodity markets. The final source of market failure is different from the others because it is normative in nature: 7. An unfair distribution of income (lack of equity).

The OCR and Edexcel AS-level specifications only require coverage of the first three of these sources of market failure and therefore you may need only to study the previous chapter and not this one, with the exception of the sections in this chapter on unstable commodity prices which are useful for all AS-level students. Those taking the AQA AS-level exam and all students of other boards progressing to A-level Year 2 should be familiar with all of the content in both Chapter 7 and Chapter 8.

Monopoly

Monopoly is an important source of market failure because economic theory predicts that monopolists will exploit their power by raising prices and restricting the quantity supplied. This results in an **inefficient allocation of resources**. AQA students should ensure that they are fully familiar with the material on monopoly in Chapter 5 on Competitive and concentrated markets, while other students will encounter this material in A-level Year 2.

Factor of production (resource) immobility

The signals of the price mechanism change when costs of production or patterns of consumer demand change. This requires resources to be reallocated, but some resources are not mobile between uses and this results in market failure in two main ways:

● **The market may not be able to respond to changes in consumer demand.** Suppose consumer demand shifted massively from Good A to Good B, for example. The market may not be able to respond to this change if the resources (land, labour, capital and enterprise) used in producing Good A could not be switched to producing Good B.

● **Resources may become unemployed if they are no longer in demand for their current use and cannot be transferred to other uses.** This is called structural unemployment. When demand for UK coal fell in the 1980s many miners were structurally unemployed as they lacked skills to work in other areas of the economy.

Unstable prices in commodity markets

Commodities are homogeneous products or materials such as agricultural produce (e.g. wheat, rice, coffee, cocoa beans), metals (e.g. copper and steel) and fuels (e.g. oil). There tends to be a single global price for commodities, determined by the forces of supply and demand.

Commodity markets are notorious for exhibiting price volatility. Prices on commodity markets fluctuate hour-by-hour and minute-by-minute and there can be periods of sharp price rises and falls. Such price volatility creates uncertainty (an example of imperfect information). This is not efficient and therefore can be considered a source of market failure. Think about the broader economic effects of sharp swings in oil prices to see why this is so.

Reasons for unstable commodity prices

1. Supply of agricultural commodities is often affected by factors beyond human control, such as weather and disease. Sudden shortages or gluts of produce result in price swings. See Figure 8.1.

2. Supply of commodities is often **inelastic** in the short term. This magnifies the effect on prices of changes in demand. See Figure 8.2.

3. Demand for some commodities can change arbitrarily. A cold winter can significantly increase the demand for oil, for example.

4. Commodities are often traded for **speculative reasons**. An expectation of price rises may cause increased demand from those hoping to make a capital gain, and this may exacerbate the extent of the price rises.

Figure 8.1: The market for coffee beans (1)

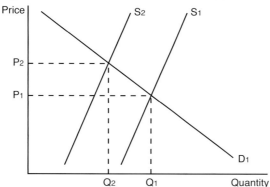

Supply shifts from S1 to S2 (for example, due to frost in Brazil affecting coffee crops).

Price rises from P1 to P2.

Quantity traded falls from Q1 to Q2.

Figure 8.2: The market for coffee beans (2)

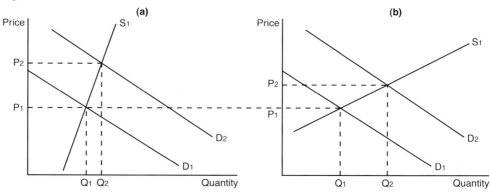

Demand increases from D1 to D2, for example because of a change in tastes towards coffee rather than tea, or because of speculative activity.

The supply of coffee beans is relatively inelastic in the short run, as in part (a) of the diagram. The resulting price increase from P1 to P2 is bigger than it would have been if supply had been more elastic as in part (b) of the diagram.

Many commodities are processed into final products. For example, coffee beans are ground and processed to make instant coffee. The prices of final products tend to be more stable than commodity prices. Taking instant coffee as an example, reasons for this include:

● Coffee beans are only a fraction of the overall costs of producing instant coffee.

● Producers of instant coffee may hold substantial stocks of beans and therefore may not be affected immediately by price fluctuations.

● Producers can insure themselves against fluctuating bean prices by taking out 'futures contracts'. These contracts guarantee the delivery of beans in the future at a price agreed today.

● Even if affected by fluctuating prices for beans, frequently changing prices for the instant coffee produced from them would carry a significant cost to producers.

A lack of equity (fairness)

The final cause of market failure is different in nature from all the others. This is why this section of text has been highlighted. The others have all been about inefficiency of resource allocation (a positive economic concept). However, many people consider that markets produce unfair outcomes and that this is also a market failure. This is a normative perspective.

Consider, for example, the distribution of income, which is largely determined in labour markets. It might be considered unfair that the top 20% of income earners enjoy as much as 50% of the national income. If so, this lack of equity constitutes a market failure and would justify government intervention to make the distribution of income more equal.

Chapter

9

Paper 1: Introductory concepts → Markets generally work well → Sometimes markets fail → **This may justify government intervention** → **Government failure sometimes occurs**

Government intervention – indirect taxation, subsidies, state provision, information provision

Government intervention

> **This box is repeated at the start of each chapter on government intervention. You are recommended to read it each time.**
>
> Government intervention is used to correct market failures arising from an inefficient resource allocation or a lack of equity.
>
> The main forms of government intervention are: 1. Indirect taxation; 2. Subsidies; 3. State provision; 4. Information provision; 5. Price controls; 6. Buffer stocks; 7. Regulation; 8. Pollution permits; 9. Extensions of property rights.
>
> Government intervention will not necessarily be **effective** in achieving its aims or succeed in improving the **efficiency** of resource allocation or improving **equity**.

Indirect taxation

(tackling market failures associated with negative externalities and demerit goods)

Indirect taxes are a tax on expenditure imposed by the government on producers. Indirect taxes are most likely to be used to reduce the number of resources allocated to the product and therefore can be used to tackle problems associated with negative externalities and demerit goods.

Indirect taxes raise a firm's costs and therefore cause an upward shift in the firm's supply curve. This means that less can be supplied at each price. A **unit tax** (or **specific tax**) will cause a **parallel shift** in the supply curve and is illustrated in Figure 9.1. The vertical distance between the supply curves shows the amount of tax per unit.

Figure 9.1

Figure 9.2

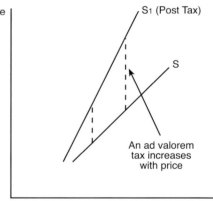

An **ad valorem** (**percentage tax**) will cause the supply curve to **tilt to the left**. This is because the size of the tax increases with price. This is illustrated in Figure 9.2. For example a 17.5% tax on £1 is 17.5p, much smaller than the same tax of £17.50 on £100.

The effects of indirect taxation on consumers and producers are dependent on the price elasticity of demand.

● In Figure 9.3 demand is **relatively price inelastic**. The producer finds it easier to pass on the tax to the consumer. The total tax per unit is ac, but the consumer pays the majority of the tax (ab) while the producer burden is bc. The quantity produced in equilibrium contracts from Q to Q_1. Total tax revenue = tax per unit (ac) x quantity traded (Q_1), and is represented by the shaded area.

Figure 9.3

Figure 9.4

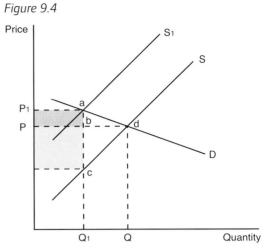

- In Figure 9.4 demand is **relatively price elastic**. The producer finds it difficult to pass on the tax to the consumer and has to **absorb** the majority of the tax itself. The producer burden (bc) outweighs the consumer burden (ab). There is a larger contraction in the quantity bought and sold – with the equilibrium quantity falling from Q to Q_1.

- When demand is inelastic the consumer faces a large price rise and, as a result, the fall in **consumer surplus** (PP_1ad) is greater than when demand is inelastic. A fall in consumer surplus will reduce consumer welfare.

Evaluating indirect taxes in tackling negative externalities and demerit goods

An indirect tax is one of the most common policies used to tackle the problems created by negative externalities. The aim of an indirect tax is to **increase the firm's costs** so that the firm is forced to take into account the external costs that it generates. It will result in a lower level of output and a more efficient allocation of resources. Examples of such taxes include: petrol tax, vehicle excise duty, landfill tax and the carbon tax.

There are however some problems in using indirect taxes to tackle negative externalities:

- Negative externalities are difficult to measure and, as a result, setting the indirect tax at the correct level is virtually impossible. In reality, therefore, all that governments and regulatory agencies can hope to achieve is a movement towards a more efficient allocation of resources.

- Indirect taxes **reduce output and raise prices**, and this will have an adverse effect on consumer welfare.

- If the aim of indirect taxation is to discourage activities that generate negative externalities, or to reduce consumption of demerit goods, the effectiveness of the policy will be reduced if demand is **inelastic**. This is a concern because there are good reasons in theory to expect demand for many demerit goods such as cigarettes and alcohol (addictive nature) and petrol (a near necessity for many aspects of modern living) to be inelastic.

- Taxes on some demerit goods may have a **regressive** effect (see Chapter 24) making the distribution of income less equal.

- If indirect taxes are raised in one country to tackle pollution, producers may shift production to countries with lower taxes. This will not reduce global pollution, and may create problems such as **unemployment and a lack of competitiveness** in the country that raised the tax.

- There may be more effective ways of improving the efficiency of resource allocation in relation to demerit goods. The effectiveness of indirect taxes should be compared against alternatives such as regulation or educating consumers about the private costs of consuming demerit goods such as cigarettes and alcohol.

● One advantage of indirect taxes is that they raise substantial revenue for the government and help fund public services.

Subsidies
(tackling market failures associated with positive externalities and merit goods)

Subsidies are **payments** made to producers by the government, which effectively reduce costs and encourage them to increase output.

The effect of a subsidy is to increase the quantity of goods sold and to reduce the market equilibrium price. Government subsidies are often offered to producers of **merit goods and services** such as public transport and industries requiring some **protection** from low cost international competition.

Figure 9.5

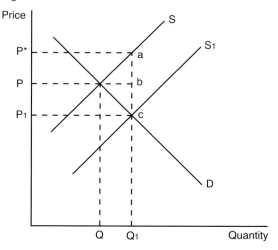

● Figure 9.5 shows a specific subsidy equal to ac per unit produced.

● The subsidy causes the firm's supply curve to shift to the right because the firm's costs are reduced.

● The total amount spent by the government on the subsidy is equal to the unit subsidy (ac) x Q_1. This is equal to the area P_1P^*ac. The consumer gain is equal to the distance (bc) while the producer gain is equal to (ab).

● The more inelastic the demand curve, the greater the fall in prices and the consumer's gain from a subsidy. Indeed when demand is totally inelastic the consumer gains the entire subsidy (but consumption does not increase at all).

Evaluating subsidies

● By increasing consumption of goods associated with positive externalities and merit goods, a subsidy may help improve **the efficiency of resource allocation**.

● The effectiveness of a subsidy in increasing consumption of a product depends on the elasticity of demand. The effectiveness of the policy is increased if demand is elastic.

● There is a danger that subsidies may support firms that are **inefficient and wasteful** in their production processes. Such firms might not survive in highly competitive markets without government support.

● Government subsidies carry an expense to the taxpayer. There is an **opportunity cost** here: the money could have been put to other uses. To spend the money on a subsidy is only sensible if it is the best use for the money.

State provision

(tackling market failures associated with merit goods and public goods)

In some cases, rather than subsidising goods, the state pays for them entirely, making them free of charge. Examples include merit goods such as education and healthcare (most NHS treatment is free of charge to patients, although there are some exceptions such as prescription charges). Public goods such as national defence and street lighting are also provided by the state.

Evaluating state provision

The points already made in relation to evaluating subsidies apply also to evaluating state provision. Note too:

● The cost of state provision is especially expensive because the good is subsidised to the point at which it is actually free of charge. Consider the huge annual cost of the NHS, for example.

● The danger of inefficient production and waste is enhanced in government run organisations, because of the lack of a profit motive.

● Governments may attempt to reduce the risk of inefficiency by financing the good free of charge to consumers and paying private sector firms to produce the service. Schools could be run by private companies, for example, in return for payment from the state. Those companies who became more efficient would increase the profits they made from the money paid to them by the government. There would be dangers, however: a drive for efficiency may reduce quality. The government would have to allocate resources to monitoring and regulating the performance of private firms running schools.

● The effectiveness of state provision in increasing consumption is likely to be limited only by the resources available. When a good or service is free of charge, economic theory suggests that any consumer who gets any utility from it at all will choose to use it. Figure 9.6 could represent the NHS. There is an excess demand for treatment and because the price is set at zero, the rationing function of prices has been suppressed. Some other way must be found of rationing available treatments. This may be 'first come first served' (NHS waiting lists!), prioritising on the basis of who needs treatment most or even the luck of the draw (the treatments available on the NHS differ in different parts of the country – the 'postcode lottery'!).

Schools could be run by private companies in return for payment from the state.

Figure 9.6

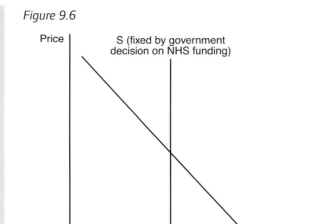

Information provision (tackling market failures of imperfect information including information failures regarding merit and demerit goods)

Governments often try to address information failures by trying to educate the public through information campaigns. Guidance on how many units of alcohol to drink tries to correct the over-consumption of a demerit good for example, while the 'five portions of fruit and vegetables a day' campaign tries to tackle the under-consumption of a merit good.

Evaluating information provision

● Information provision is potentially very effective because it directly tackles the problem causing the market failure. In theory, if information campaigns are effective, the problem of imperfect information will no longer exist.

● However, there is no guarantee that the public will take notice of information campaigns or adjust their behaviour. They may be addicted, for example, to alcohol or cigarettes, and this **habitual behaviour** may not change even if information gaps are filled.

● Information campaigns carry an expense to the taxpayer. There is an **opportunity cost** as the money could have been spent elsewhere. To spend the money on information provision is only sensible if this is the best use for the money.

Chapter
10

Paper 1: Introductory concepts → Markets generally work well → Sometimes markets fail → **This may justify government intervention** → **Government failure sometimes occurs**

Government intervention – price controls, buffer stocks

Government intervention

This box is repeated at the start of each chapter on government intervention. You are recommended to read it each time.

Government intervention is used to correct market failures arising from an inefficient resource allocation or a lack of equity.

The main forms of government intervention are: 1. Indirect taxation; 2. Subsidies; 3. State provision; 4. Information provision; 5. Price controls; 6. Buffer stocks; 7. Regulation; 8. Pollution permits; 9. Extensions of property rights.

Government intervention will not necessarily be **effective** in achieving its aims or succeed in improving the **efficiency** of resource allocation or improving **equity**.

Price controls

Governments can intervene to impose legally binding price controls on a market, in the form of a maximum or minimum price.

Maximum prices
(tackling a lack of equity for consumers)

A maximum price is a **price ceiling**. To be effective, it must be set below the market equilibrium. A maximum price set above the equilibrium has no effect on the market.

A maximum price might be used to tackle a market failure arising from a lack of equity. It might be considered unfair that some goods are not sufficiently affordable to consumers. Indeed, some **firms** voluntarily set maximum prices for their products for this reason. The price for sell out sports fixtures and concerts is below the equilibrium. Part of the reason for this is the **equity** consideration of ensuring that fans are not priced out of the market by corporate hospitality and the rich.

Figure 10.1 shows a maximum price. Because the price ceiling is set at P_1, there will be a contraction of market supply and expansion of market demand leading to a shortage (**excess demand**) in the market equal to Q_1-Q_2.

Figure 10.1

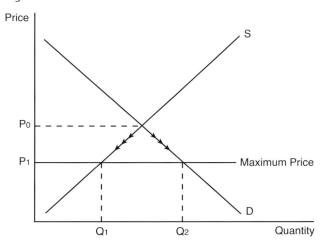

Evaluating maximum prices

The excess demand created by a maximum price cannot be cleared because the **rationing function** (see Chapter 5) of prices has been suppressed. This means that there must be some other way of rationing the product. Options include:

1. 'First come first served' (queuing). This is a particularly inefficient option, taking up the time of people stuck in the queue. Consider traffic jams, caused by queues for road space!

2. Seller's preference (the seller chooses to whom they sell the product, for example loyal customers).

3. Lucky ballot (random selection of who gets to buy the product).

● It is a **normative** (subjective opinion) based consideration as to whether a maximum price improves fairness. However, it might be noted that the excess demand means that some people who are willing to pay for the product are not able to make a purchase.

● It may prove difficult to suppress the functioning of the free market and it is possible that the shortage may lead to a black market developing. This means that the product may still be rationed by price to an extent, with those willing to pay more receiving the good.

● Thus, to make a maximum price scheme effective, the authorities must spend resources to discourage **black markets** (detecting and punishing those who purchase at the maximum price to sell on to others at a profit).

Minimum prices
(tackling a lack of equity for suppliers)

A minimum price is a **price floor**. To be effective it must be set above the market equilibrium. A minimum price set below the equilibrium has no effect on the market.

The reason for setting a minimum price would normally be to ensure that suppliers receive what is considered to be a fair price, thus guaranteeing them a decent standard of living. Minimum prices are common in agriculture. The national minimum wage is another well known example of a minimum price.

Figure 10.2 shows a minimum price. If the minimum price is set at P_1, there will be an excess supply equal to Q_2-Q_1. This is because the above equilibrium price causes demand to contract and supply to expand.

Figure 10.2

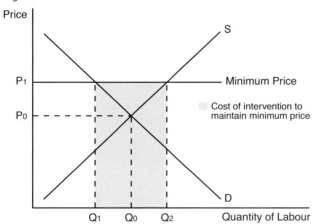

Evaluating minimum prices

● It is a **normative** consideration as to whether any particular minimum price improves fairness. Note, however, that consumers pay higher prices than they would in the absence of government intervention.

● The minimum price may be influenced by political pressure on the part of producers who stand to benefit from higher prices. This may create conflict between political and economic objectives, a potential source of **government failure** (see Chapter 12).

● To maintain a minimum price it is likely that the governing authorities will have to buy up the excess supply at the agreed minimum price (this is called **intervention buying**). The cost of doing this is represented by the shaded area in Figure 10.2. This expense carries an opportunity cost, as the money could have been spent on other projects. Might some of these projects have been a better use of the money?

● Once purchased, the excess supply is likely to be destroyed. This constitutes a waste of scarce resources. It would be more efficient to pay producers to do nothing than to use resources to produce output that will be destroyed!

Buffer stocks
(tackling market failure due to price instability in commodity markets)

An understanding of buffer stocks as a method of government intervention is only explicitly required for AS-level by the OCR specification.

A buffer stock is used to stabilise prices of a product in the face of fluctuating supply and to prevent the periodic shortages that are seen in many commodity markets.

Figure 10.3 illustrates the working of a buffer stock scheme. Many commodities have inelastic supply in the short run, and the diagram assumes for simplicity that supply is totally inelastic.

In periods of high supply (see S_1 in Figure 10.3) the government engages in intervention buying (quantity bc) to maintain the target price. This supply is stored, and is released back onto the market if needed at a later date. In periods of shortage (S_2) quantity ab is released from the buffer stock, thereby preventing prices from rising.

Figure 10.3

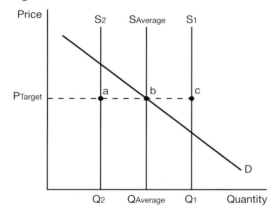

Evaluating buffer stocks

● Buffer stocks can in theory be self-financing. If the price is set at the long run average, the money spent on intervention buying during periods of surplus is recovered when the buffer stock is released at a later date. The **stabilisation** of the price helps improve efficiency.

● However, the above point ignores the costs of administering the scheme and storing the buffer stock. Also, there may be waste as some commodities are perishable and cannot be stored indefinitely.

● The target price is often set above the long run average due to political pressure from producers. This makes the scheme in effect a minimum price scheme, with the expense and waste that this might imply, while raising questions about **equity**, because consumers face higher prices.

● Buffer stocks may struggle to stabilise the price if any major producers are not part of the scheme. During periods of surplus, other producers are likely to undercut the target price of the buffer stock scheme.

● Empirical evidence suggests that buffer stocks have often not been effective in stabilising prices.

Chapter

11

Paper 1: Introductory concepts → Markets generally work well → Sometimes markets fail → **This may justify government intervention** → **Government failure sometimes occurs**

Government intervention – regulation, extending property rights, tradable pollution permits

Government intervention

> **This box is repeated at the start of each chapter on government intervention. You are recommended to read it each time.**

> Government intervention is used to correct market failures arising from an inefficient resource allocation or a lack of equity.
>
> The main forms of government intervention are: 1. Indirect taxation; 2. Subsidies; 3. State provision; 4. Information provision; 5. Price controls; 6. Buffer stocks; 7. Regulation; 8. Pollution permits; 9. Extensions of property rights.
>
> Government intervention will not necessarily be **effective** in achieving its aims or succeed in improving the **efficiency** of resource allocation or improving **equity**.

Regulation (tackling the market failures of monopoly power, negative externalities and demerit goods)

Governments sometimes seek to tackle market failures by putting into place legal restrictions (regulations) on the behaviour of firms and consumers. For example:

Regulating monopoly power
● In the UK, the Competition and Markets Authority is empowered to investigate mergers and takeovers and block them if they think the mergers and takeovers will result in excessive monopoly power.

● The Competition and Markets Authority also investigates and remedies anti-competitive practices such as cartels and other price fixing agreements. Firms can be fined up to 10% of turn over and company directors jailed for price fixing.

● Permanent regulatory bodies oversee the conduct of firms providing household utilities such as water, gas and electricity. For example, OFWAT has the power to cap the prices charged by the regional water monopolies.

Regulating demerit goods
● Some drugs are illegal.

● There are age restrictions on who can buy alcohol and cigarettes.

● Smoking is not allowed in enclosed public spaces.

Regulating negative externalities (such as pollution)
● The enforcement of minimum environmental standards is common in many industries, in order to protect air and water quality and restrict emissions of green house gases.

● Firms can be fined if their production processes emit pollution in excess of the legally permitted levels.

Evaluating regulation	● Regulations must be enforced and this carries an **administrative cost**. There is an opportunity cost in devoting scarce resources to the process of regulation. High administrative costs are a potential source of **government failure** (see Chapter 12), as is the next issue, a lack of information.

● The success of regulation depends partly on the quality of information available to regulators. For example, it is difficult to judge the optimal levels of pollution because it is difficult to place a monetary value on negative externalities. A further example is that utility regulators attempt to set the price much as it would be in a competitive market, but may lack the information to judge this accurately.

● Note the optimal level of pollution is unlikely to be zero, because this would imply zero economic activity.

● Regulation of negative externalities in production attempts to force all firms to cut their emissions to the legally allowed level. Some firms will find it very costly (**inefficient**) to do so, but the law will still attempt to enforce this.

● There may be superior policies available. For example, in the field of negative externalities, the policies of **extending property rights** and allocating **tradable pollution permits** are highly regarded. **Negative externalities** could also be tackled by indirect taxation.

Extending property rights
(tackling market failure associated with negative externalities in production)

Negative externalities arise largely from the fact that nobody owns the environment and it is therefore free to use.

Consider the example of a chemical factory that discharges its waste products into a local river. This kills some fish, negatively affecting third parties in the form of the local fishing club who use the river.

Allocating ownership of the river to the fishing club would produce an efficient outcome. Where the benefit to the chemical company of polluting the river exceeded the cost to the fishing club of allowing that pollution, the chemical company would be able to compensate the fishing club and both parties would be better off. This would work the other way round if ownership of the river was given to the chemical firm. In either case, all mutually beneficial trades would be undertaken and the socially optimal level of pollution found.

Evaluating the extension of property rights

● The extension of property rights is a theoretically simple method of achieving an efficient economic outcome, as analysed above.

● The externality is successfully **internalised** (brought back within the market system). If the fishing club own the river, the chemical company is forced to pay for the pollution it generates.

● There is no need for regulatory authorities to try to make artificial judgements about the optimal level of pollution.

● For these reasons, extending property rights is often thought to be an effective and superior alternative to regulating pollution.

● However, it will be necessary to legally protect the property rights of the owners of environmental resources. This itself carries a cost and may be difficult (could the polluting activities of the chemical company be accurately measured and checked against levels that have been agreed with the fishing club?)

● There are **equity** considerations. The optimal level of pollution will be found regardless of who is allocated ownership of the river, but this decision affects the **distribution of income and wealth**: you are better off if you own something than if you don't. An option is for the government to auction the property rights in the first instance, thereby generating revenue.

Regulation of negative externalities in production attempts to force all firms to cut their emissions to the legally allowed level.

Marketable pollution permits

An alternative to full allocation of property rights is for governments to cap pollution at what they judge to be the optimal level. Firms are then allocated permits to allow them to emit a certain level of pollution in an agreed time period (say a year) but can sell any permits that they do not need to other firms. Such '**emissions trading**' or '**cap and trade**' schemes have become increasingly prominent and have been extended to international agreements, where countries have permits to produce agreed levels of pollution but can sell these permits to other countries if they wish.

Evaluating marketable pollution permits

● The key advantage of pollution permits is that those firms or countries who find it least costly to control pollution will do so and then sell their spare permits to those who find it most expensive. The most efficient way of reaching the desired level of pollution is therefore found.

● International cap and trade schemes can be used to address injustices in the international distribution of income. If poor countries are allocated sufficient permits, they can sell them to richer countries who wish to carry on polluting. The effect is that the richer countries compensate the poorer for the pollution generated.

● As with the allocation of property rights, what was previously an externality (outside the market) has been **internalised** and those who pollute now have to pay for their activities.

● However, the scheme does require a judgement to be reached about the optimal level of pollution. Such a judgement is incredibly difficult to make.

● A new market in pollution permits has been created and this market itself may be subject to **market failures**.

● The trading of permits affects the geographical distribution of pollution. Some pollutants may cause more damage if they are heavily concentrated in one geographical area, rather than being more widely spread.

Chapter

12

Paper 1: Introductory concepts → Markets generally work well → Sometimes markets fail → This may justify government intervention → **Government failure sometimes occurs**

Government failure

Government failure

Government failure occurs when government intervention imposes a cost greater than the benefits brought about through the intervention. Thus the government intervention itself causes a **misallocation of resources** and a net loss of **economic welfare**.

It is difficult to prove that any particular policy is an example of government failure. However, we can use economic theory and empirical ('real world') evidence to suggest cases where it as at least possible that government failure has occurred.

Sources of government failure

The main sources of government failure are:

- **Inadequate information** about the extent of the market failure being tackled and the consequences of the policy.

- **Unintended consequences** – government interventions often have unwanted side-effects.

- **Conflicting objectives** – this could be conflict between different economic objectives or conflict between political and economic objectives.

- The **administrative costs** of the policy.

Inadequate information

The extent of many market failures is difficult to identify, making it difficult to intervene appropriately. Consider the following examples:

- To what extent would education be under provided in the free market? What level of funding from the government would help bring about an optimal resource allocation?

- How much alcohol consumption is optimal? The answer is probably not zero, given that people do derive utility from consumption and that there are benefits in terms of social interaction.

- What is the optimal level of carbon dioxide emissions? Again, the answer is almost certainly not zero given that this would imply ceasing all activities which generate emissions.

It is clear from the above points that it is not possible to have information to give definitive answers to these questions. Governments also lack clear information about the effects of their policies, which sometimes cause **unintended consequences**. For example:

- Tightening environmental regulations for firms may simply lead them to locate elsewhere, where regulation is loose or does not exist at all. Taxing firms for polluting may have similar effects. The net effect may be more damage to the environment.

- Regulation to prohibit drug use means that users can only purchase drugs on the black market. This means they cannot have full knowledge of the nature of the drugs they buy. Impure drugs may lead to severe health problems or death. The high price of addictive drugs on the black market may also cause users to turn to crime in order to finance their habit, generating negative externalities.

- Raising taxes on demerit goods may cause consumers to buy them from countries where taxes are lower, thus the policy may not be effective in lowering consumption, but may lead to a reduction of government revenue.

- Government organisations, such as regulatory bodies and the NHS, are notorious for waste, using the resources given to them inefficiently because of the absence of the profit motive.

In all the cases of unintended consequences above, government intervention has encouraged economic agents to behave in an undesirable way. The intervention has thus distorted the market by creating undesirable incentives.

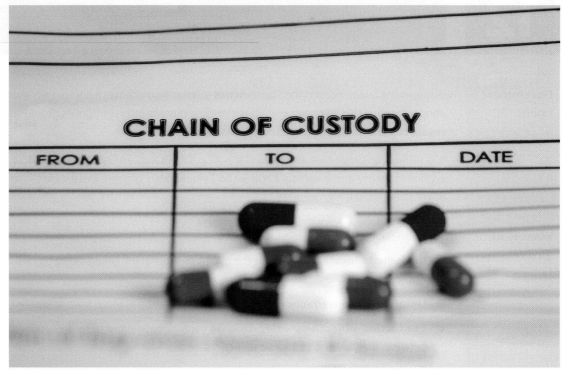

A ban on the sale and use of drugs would require policing.

Conflicting objectives

Governments have numerous economic objectives and these may sometimes come into conflict with each other. For example, government intervention to improve **equity** frequently distorts economic incentives and may cause **inefficiency**. The availability of benefits may reduce the incentive to work, for instance. This is one case of what is known as the **equity-efficiency trade-off**.

Political objectives and considerations may also interfere with economic policy making. For instance, the intervention buying price in minimum price or buffer stock schemes is often set too high due to pressure from producers. This serves to raise prices to consumers and leads to the production of excess supply which may have to be destroyed, wasting resources.

Governments may also be tempted to put into place policies which make them popular in the short term but may be economically damaging in the long term. At a macro level, expansionary monetary and fiscal policy in the run up to elections may cause problems in the future. This makes a case for independent policy making, for example central banks having the power to set interest rates. At a micro level, subsidising a failing industry is popular with those who depend on it for a livelihood but is not necessarily economically efficient.

The administrative costs of policy

The administrative costs of a policy can sometimes be substantial and may contribute to a situation where the policy as a whole carries costs in excess of the benefits. Examples of the administrative costs of policy include:

● The cost of enforcing regulations. A ban on the sale and use of drugs for example, requires policing and cases must be brought before the courts for those caught.

● The resources used in the process of policy making may themselves be substantial. For example, in setting a price cap for the water industry OFWAT must undertake substantial research, using significant labour resources.

● Wasted resources due to the lack of a profit motive in the public sector. Given the opportunity, the private sector may produce more health care than the public sector using the same resources, for example.

Chapter

13

Paper 2: Measuring the macroeconomy → How the macroeconomy works →
Macroeconomic performance → Macroeconomic policy tools

Macroeconomic indicators and objectives

Macro-economic indicators

Macroeconomics deals with the performance of the economy as a whole. The four main indicators used to measure macroeconomic performance are:

● Economic growth (measured via national income)

● Unemployment

● Inflation

● The current account of the balance of payments.

Macro-economic objectives

Governments have objectives in relation to each of these four key variables, preferring **strong and sustainable economic growth, low unemployment, low and stable inflation and an acceptable balance of payments position** (this may imply avoiding large and persistent deficits).

Other government objectives may include achieving greater income equality, protecting the environment and balancing the budget so that government spending is equal to taxation revenue.

Calculating and interpreting index numbers

Data on economic indicators are often presented in **index form**. Index numbers can be used to make a comparison between the values taken by a given variable in different time periods. The index is assigned a value of 100 in the base period and the values in other time periods are expressed relative to this. Index numbers do not have units.

Index numbers can be calculated using the following formula:

Index number = (Value in current period/value in base period) x 100

If, for example, a train ticket for travel from Nottingham to London was priced at £50 in 2016 but was priced at £40 two years earlier in 2014, then the index number for the price of the ticket in 2016 with 2014 as the base is:

Index = (£50/£40) x 100 = 125

When interpreting data presented in index form, it is important to be aware of the base. A sub-title to a graph of 2015 = 100, for example, tells us that the data is in index form with 2015 as the base. On occasion, the base may not be a time period. Where the intention is to allow easy comparison between the UK and other countries, for example, data such as GDP figures might be presented in index form with the sub-heading of the graph as UK = 100.

The change in an index number between one time period and another is only a percentage change if comparing a given time period directly to the base period. Suppose that the index number for the price of internet subscriptions was 120 in 2015 and 132 in 2016 with 2012 as the base. The percentage increase between 2015 and 2016 is calculated as:

% change = (Absolute change in index value/original index value) x 100

% change = (132-120/120) x 100 = (12/120) x 100 = 10%

Care should be taken when comparing indices for two different variables. Suppose, for example, that the price of second hand cars went up by 10% between 2015 and 2016, while the price of new cars went up only 5%. The index for the price of second hand cars in 2016 (2015=100) would be higher at 110 than that for new cars at 105. However, it is clearly **not** true that the price of second hand cars was higher in

2016 than in 2015; simply that the price of second hand cars had risen at a faster rate between the two years.

Details on how to calculate a **weighted price index** for a basket of goods are included in the section on measuring inflation later in this chapter.

Measuring economic growth

Economic growth is measured as the change in national income over time.

The main measure of national income is **Gross Domestic Product** (**GDP**). This is defined as the value of output produced within the domestic boundaries of the UK over a period of time, usually a year. It includes the output of foreign firms that are located in the UK, such as Nissan in Sunderland. It does not include the output of UK firms that are located abroad.

An alternative measure of national income is **Gross National Product** (**GNP**), also known as **Gross National Income** (**GNI**). It measures the value of income from UK owned factors of production over a given period of time, usually a year. GNP is concerned with the income generated by UK owned factors of production regardless of whether they are located in the UK or overseas. It excludes the output of foreign firms located in the UK, but includes the output of UK firms located abroad.

> **GNI = GDP + Net property income from abroad (NPIA)**

Net property income from abroad is the net balance of **interest, profits and dividends** (**IPD**) coming into the UK from UK assets owned overseas matched against the outflow of profits and other incomes from foreign owned assets located within the UK. For example, if a British-owned company operating in Germany sends some of its profits back to the UK this adds to UK GNI. Similarly, when a Japanese company located in the UK sends profits to Japan this will reduce UK GNI.

It is important to know that it is true by identity (definition) that national income, output and expenditure are equal to one another:

> **National Output = National Income = National Expenditure**

This is most easily understood using the **circular flow of income**, as explained in Chapter 14.

Measuring unemployment

The unemployed are those of a working age who are actively seeking work but do not have a job. Working age is defined as 16-65 for males, with the female retirement age in the process of being raised from 60 to 65. By 2046, the working age will be 16-68 for both males and females.

Unemployment is a **stock** concept: it measures the number of people who are out of work at a given period of time. However, each month workers lose their jobs while others find new employment. Unemployment will fall if the **flow** of workers finding employment is greater than the number of workers losing their jobs.

The claimant count measure of unemployment simply counts the numbers claiming unemployment related benefit.

The **Labour Force Survey (LFS) method** is based on a quarterly survey of 40,000 households and 100,000 individuals and uses the International Labour Organisation (ILO) definition of unemployment. It covers those who have looked for work in the past four weeks and are available to start work in the next two weeks.

Problems with the claimant count include:

● It is open to manipulation by politicians, as they can change the rules on who is entitled to claim benefits.

- It may understate unemployment because not everyone entitled to claim benefit does so.

- It may understate unemployment because some unemployed people are not entitled to benefit, for example if their spouse is in well paid employment.

- It may overstate unemployment because some people claim benefit fraudulently.

- Part-time workers who wish to work full time are not included in the statistics. These workers are classed as **underemployed**. This is a problem that is common to the claimant count and LFS (ILO) method.

Measuring inflation

Inflation is a persistent increase in the general level of prices over time.

The main measures of inflation are the Retail Price Index (RPI) and the government's preferred measure, the Consumer Price Index (CPI).

Retail Price Index (RPI)

- The RPI measures the **average** change in prices of a representative sample ('basket') of around 700 goods and services.

- Each month, a market research company collects over 180,000 separate price samples. These are then used to compile the inflation statistics which measure the change in prices over the preceeding 12 months.

- The index is **weighted** according to the proportion of income spent by the average household on categories of goods and services, such as food and housing. The weights are determined by the Expenditure and Food Survey that samples around 7000 households each year. Certain households are excluded from the survey. These include those households within the top 4% of incomes and pensioners. These groups are excluded to make the RPI more representative of the average household.

- The goods included in the index are changed over time to reflect changing consumer spending habits. In 2015, e-cigarettes and streaming music subscriptions were included for the first time.

- The weights are amended periodically to reflect changing spending patterns in the economy. The weight attached to leisure items tends to increase if the economy grows, because leisure spending is income elastic.

Other measures of inflation centred on the RPI include:

- The **RPIX**, which excludes mortgage interest payments.

- The **RPIY**, which excludes mortgage interest payments and indirect taxes.

Consumer Price Index (CPI)

The CPI is calculated using essentially the same price data as the RPI, but differs from it in some key respects. The differences include:

- the goods and services covered by the index. For instance, the CPI does not include Council Tax and a number of other housing costs faced by homeowners.

- the people whose expenditure is covered by the weights. The CPI covers a broader section of the population than the RPI.

- the mathematical formulae used to calculate the price changes in the two indices differ. This means that the CPI always shows a lower inflation rate than the RPI for any given set of price data.

| **Calculating a weighted price index** | Greater understanding of the RPI and CPI can be gained from following the calculation in a simplified example. Suppose that the basket of goods and services contains only five items: New cars, bread, milk, newspapers and beer. Consumers spend 40% of their income on new cars, 20% on bread, 20% on milk and 10% each on newspapers and beer. |

Separate indices are constructed for each item based on the price change between Years 1 and 2, as shown in Table 13.1. A simple index can then be calculated by taking the mean of the separate indices for the five items. In the example, this gives an inflation rate between Years 1 and 2 of 5.6%. A more accurate measure of inflation, however, recognises patterns of consumer expenditure. Each separate index is multiplied by a weight reflecting the proportion of expenditure accounted for by the item. The resulting figures are summed and divided by the number of weights used. This gives an inflation rate of 4.3%.

Table 13.1

Year 1 = 100

Item	Price Year 1	Price Year 2	Calculation for index in Year 2	Index Year 2	Weight	Weighted Index Year 2
New cars	£15000	£14250	(£14250/£15000) x 100	95	4	4x95 = 380
Bread	£1.40/loaf	£1.68/loaf	(£1.68/£1.40) x 100	120	2	2x120 = 240
Milk	£0.50/pint	£0.55/pint	(£0.55/£0.50) x 100	110	2	2x110 = 220
Newspapers	£0.50	£0.50	(£0.50/£0.50) x 100	100	1	1x100 = 100
Beer	£3.00/pint	£3.09pint	(£3.09/£3.00) x 100	103	1	1x103 = 103
Index for basket:				528/5 = **105.6**		1043/10 = **104.3**

| **Measuring the current account of the balance of payments** | The current account primarily measures net trade in goods and services. |

The current account is composed of four sections:

Trade in goods including items such as:

- Manufactured goods
- Semi-finished goods and components
- Energy products
- Raw materials
- Consumer goods and capital goods

Transfers. In the UK's case, we transfer significant money to the EU each year and also make foreign aid payments.

Trade in services including items such as:

- Banking, insurance and consultancy
- Tourism
- Transport and shipping
- Education
- Cultural arts

International flows of wages, interest, profit and dividends.

The current account records the **flow of money** between countries, not the movement of goods and services. For example, the sale of a UK produced car to France (an export) would result in a flow of money into the UK, and this would, therefore, be represented as a **plus sign** in the current account. The fact that the car leaves the UK is irrelevant. Similarly if a UK consumer buys insurance from a German firm (an import), this would result in a flow of money out of the UK and would be represented as a **minus sign** in the current account.

The two main elements in the current account are:

- The **trade in goods section**, or visible balance, records trade in tangible products. Over recent decades the UK has had a **visible deficit**. This means that the **value of imported goods** exceeds the

value of exported goods. For example, if the value of imported goods is £100bn and the value of exported goods is £70bn, then the trade in goods, or visible deficit, would be £30bn.

● The **trade in services section**, or invisible balance, measures trade in intangible services. The UK has traditionally experienced an **invisible surplus**. This means that the **value of exported services** exceeds the **value of imported services**. For example, if the value of exported services is £50bn and the value of imported services is £40bn, then the trade in services, or invisible surplus, would be £10bn.

The UK has run a current account deficit for many years as the invisible surplus has been insufficient to match the visible deficit.

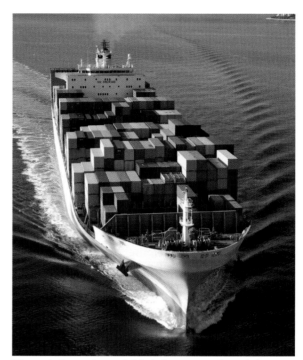

The trade in goods, or visible balance, records trade in tangible products.

Measuring the capital and financial accounts of the balance of payments

Only the OCR specification explicitly requires knowledge of these sections of the Balance of Payments for AS Level. However, other students will encounter this material in A-level Year 2.

The **capital account** records the following:

● Flows of real direct investment (for example, a foreign car manufacturer building a plant in the UK would create a credit on the capital account).

● Portfolio investment (for example, a citizen of another country buying shares in a UK firm would create a credit).

● Cross-border loans (for example, a UK firm borrowing money from a bank in another country would create a credit).

A good way to distinguish capital account entries from current account ones is that capital account entries create **assets or liabilities**. All of the inflows of money to the UK covered in the examples above would create liabilities, leading to debits on the current account at some future date. For instance, profits from the foreign car manufacturer are likely to be remitted to the firm's country of origin, creating debits on the wages, interest, profit and dividends section of the current account.

The **financial account** shows changes to assets held by the central bank of the country, in the UK's case the Bank of England. Foreign currency reserves are an example. If the Bank of England were to see a fall in its foreign currency reserves this is treated, somewhat counter-intuitively, as a credit on the financial account.

By definition, the Balance of Payments must sum to zero. If there is a deficit on the UK current account, the capital and financial accounts must combine to give a credit of equal value. In essence, the capital and current accounts show where the foreign currency to finance a current account deficit is obtained from, or how any surplus on the current account is used. Due to administrative errors in the accounts it is usually necessary to include a figure called a balancing item to ensure that the accounts do actually sum to zero.

Chapter

14

Paper 2: Measuring the macroeconomy → **How the macroeconomy works** →
Macroeconomic performance → Macroeconomic policy tools

The circular flow of income and aggregate demand (AD)

The circular flow of income

The circular flow model looks at the interaction between members of households and firms.

Members of households supply **factors of production to firms**, receiving income (**factor payments**) in return. The various factor payments are shown below:

Factor	Payment
Land	Rent
Labour	Wages and salaries
Capital	Interest
Enterprise	Profit

The firms combine the factors of production into **output**, which households spend their money on. This is known as **expenditure**. Firms then return this money to households in the next round of factor payments (**income**), setting up a circular flow.

The circular flow helps us to understand the national income identity:

National output = National income = National expenditure

The income received by households funds the expenditure on the output produced by firms. Income, output and expenditure are thus the same flow measured at three different points.

Note also that:

● Households do not spend all of their income. They save some at banks and other financial institutions. This money can be lent out to firms for investment projects.

● The government sector is also important through their taxation and spending decisions.

● There is spending on imported goods and services and injections of demand into the economy from the sale of exports.

The circular flow is shown in Figure 14.1.

Figure 14.1

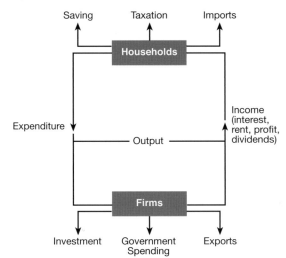

Injections and withdrawals

The circular flow of income highlights the main injections and withdrawals in an economy.

Injections	Withdrawals
Exports (X)	Imports (M)
Investment (I)	Savings (S)
Government spending (G)	Taxation (T)

Injections will add money to the circular flow of income while withdrawals will remove money from it. If **injections are greater than withdrawals**, expenditure on goods and services will exceed the planned level of production. Firms will, therefore, expand output and **national income will rise**. Conversely if **withdrawals are greater than injections**, production will exceed the current level of expenditure. Firms will, therefore, reduce their output and **national income will fall**.

The aggregate demand curve

Aggregate Demand is the **total spending on goods and services** in an economy over a given period of time. It is calculated using the following formula:

**AD = Consumer expenditure (C) + Investment (I)
+ Government expenditure (G) + (Exports (X) – Imports (M))**

C **Consumer spending** – is spending on goods and services that are used for the **direct satisfaction** of individual or collective needs. It is also known as **household final consumption expenditure**. This includes personal expenditure on durable and non-durable goods, as well as on services.

I **Gross Domestic Fixed Capital Formation** – is investment spending on assets that are used repeatedly or continuously over a number of years to produce goods. For example, spending by companies on **capital goods** such as machinery and vehicles. Investment also includes spending on **working capital** such as **stocks** of finished goods and work in progress.

G **General Government Final Consumption** – is current spending on publicly provided goods and services. It also includes spending on public sector employment.

X **Exports of goods and services** – this is UK produced output that is sold abroad. Exports are an **injection** into the circular flow of income.

M **Imports of goods and services** – this is foreign produced output that is purchased by UK consumers and firms. Imports are a **withdrawal** from the circular flow of income.

Figure 14.2

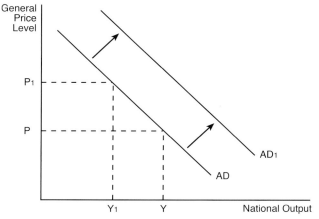

Figure 14.2 illustrates an **aggregate demand curve**. It is very much like an ordinary demand curve, but the axes on the diagram are different. National output is placed on the x-axis and the general price level is represented on the y-axis.

The AD curve is **downward sloping**. A rise in the price level from P to P₁ will lead to a fall in the total demand for goods and services from Y to Y₁. This is because:

● at higher price levels the total demand for goods and services will be lower.

● as the price level becomes higher, British goods become **less competitive**. Higher imports and lower exports will reduce AD.

A number of factors will cause the AD curve to shift:

● The **aggregate demand curve** will shift to the **right** from AD to AD₁ when there is a rise in **consumption**, or any of the three injections into the circular flow of income, namely **investment**, **government spending or exports**.

● A **rise in imports** will shift the **aggregate demand curve to the left**. This is because imports are a withdrawal from the circular flow of income and will reduce the total demand for UK goods and services.

For example:

Event	AD shift	Explanation
Income tax cut	Right	The income tax cut will increase disposable income, boosting consumption.
Interest rate rise	Left	A higher interest rate raises the opportunity cost of spending (saving more attractive, borrowing expensive). Consumption and investment both fall.
An increase in the budget deficit	Right	Government spending has risen relative to taxation. The government provides a bigger net injection to the circular flow.
A stronger pound	Left	The stronger pound makes imports cheaper and exports more expensive. Net exports (X-M) fall.
An increase in the general price level	AD does **not** shift but does contract	Changes in the general price level cause a movement along the AD curve.

The factors that influence the components of aggregate demand will be analysed more fully in later chapters.

Remember that a change in the general price level will not itself shift the AD curve. The general price level is on the y-axis and thus varies along the length of the curve. A change in the general price level would create an extension or a contraction of AD rather than a shift of the curve.

The multiplier effect

An initial injection into the circular flow of income will cause a greater change in aggregate demand and national income.

The multiplier is defined as the ratio of the change in national income to the change in expenditure that brought it about.

Many examples can be used to illustrate the multiplier. Most importantly you must be able to describe in simple terms the **multiplier process**. Consider the effects of an increase in investment by a firm on new machines of £100m. This will raise national income by £100m since the **expenditure of one group is the income of another**. The process will not stop here though. The initial expenditure will **generate incomes** that will be used to finance spending in future time periods. This adds to the effects on total GDP.

At each stage of the process, as income is earned through additional spending, some will leak out of the circular flow of income in the form of **savings** (incomes not spent), **taxation** (taken out by the Government sector) and **imports** (the demand for foreign produced goods and services). Thus the **size of the multiplier effect** is determined by the **rate of leakages or withdrawals from the economy**. The multiplier in a modern economy tends to be small. This is largely because modern economies are open to trade and a considerable proportion of spending is on imports, which serve to reduce the value of the multiplier as they are a leakage from the circular flow.

The size and calculation of the multiplier

The multiplier (K) can be calculated as the ratio of the change in national income (GDP) to the injection (J) that brought it about:

K = ΔGDP/J (where Δ denotes 'change in')

For example, if a £2bn investment gives rise to a £5bn increase in GDP, then the size of the multiplier is 2.5, calculated as:

K = £5bn/£2.5bn = 2.5

Those studying the Edexcel and OCR AS-level courses may also need to calculate the multiplier using the concept of the **marginal propensity to consume**. This is the proportion of each additional pound of income that consumers spend on UK produced goods and services. Similarly, the **marginal propensity to save** measures the proportion of each additional pound of income which is saved, while there are corresponding concepts for the other withdrawals from the circular flow (the **marginal rate of tax**, sometimes known as the marginal propensity to tax, and the **marginal propensity to import**). By definition, these marginal propensities must sum to one as they collectively show what happens to each pound of income.

The value of the multiplier can be calculated as:

K = 1/(1-MPC) or K = 1/MPW

(where MPC is the marginal propensity to consumer and MPW is the marginal propensity to withdraw, consisting of the marginal propensities to save and import and the marginal rate of tax)

Suppose in a given economy, the following figures apply:

Marginal propensity to consume = 0.4

Marginal propensity to save = 0.1

Marginal rate of tax = 0.3

Marginal propensity to import = 0.2

The multiplier can thus be calculated as:

K = 1/(1-0.4) or K =1/0.6

K = 1.67 (an injection of £1bn to the circular flow will create £1.67bn of national income)

[Mathematicians may recognise this as the summing of an infinite geometric progression. Of the initial injection of £1bn, only £0.4bn stays in the circular flow of income as expenditure with the rest leaking from the system as withdrawals. At the next stage only 0.4 of this £0.4bn (£0.16bn) stays within the circular flow, then 0.4 of £0.16bn and so on. Each term in the series is derived by multiplying the previous term by 0.4]

Chapter

15

Paper 2: Measuring the macroeconomy → **How the macroeconomy works** → Macroeconomic performance → Macroeconomic policy tools

Aggregate supply (AS) and macroeconomic equilibrium

Classical short run aggregate supply (SRAS)

Aggregate supply is the total volume of goods and services that domestic firms are willing and able to supply over a given period of time and at a given general price level.

The AQA AS-level specification is based on the Classical short and long run aggregate supply curves outlined in the following sections. Students of the Edexcel and OCR specifications should be aware of both the Classical and Keynesian views of aggregate supply.

The short run is defined here as the period of time in which the prices of factors of production (and hence the costs of production) are fixed.

Like microeconomic supply curves, the short run aggregate supply curve (SRAS) slopes upwards from left to right. This is because the SRAS curve is drawn for a given cost of production, and thus any rise in the general price level increases profit margins encouraging an extension of supply.

Any change in production costs will shift the SRAS curve. Thus the curve would shift in response to changes to payments to any factors of production or in response to changes to their productivity.

For example:

Event	SRAS Shift	Explanation
Rise in oil prices	Left	Oil is important in many industrial processes and for transport of goods. Higher costs of production reduce profit margins.
Fall in wages	Right	Falling **unit labour costs** (labour costs/divided by output).
Higher labour productivity	Right	More is produced in each hour worked. Assuming wages are constant, unit labour costs fall.
A stronger pound	Right	The stronger pound makes the price of imported raw materials cheaper, lowering production costs.
A fall in the general price level	SRAS does not shift but does contract	Changes in the general price level cause a movement along the SRAS curve.

Those factors that reduced production costs in the table above lead to an increase of SRAS (a rightwards shift) as illustrated in Figure 15.1

Figure 15.1

Classical long run aggregate supply (LRAS)

In the long run, the prices of factors of production can change. Classical economists assume that they adjust to bring about equilibrium in the markets for factors of production; thus in the long run resources will be fully employed and the economy will operate at full productive potential (capacity) regardless of the general price level in the economy. Hence the long run aggregate supply curve (LRAS) can be drawn as vertical.

The productive potential of an economy is determined by the factors of production available to it. This means that the quantity and quality (productivity) of the economy's land, labour, capital and enterprise determine the position of the long run aggregate supply curve.

Accordingly, LRAS would increase or shift right through a range of factors such as technological advances, improved education and skills, greater participation in the labour market (for example through delayed retirement), inwards migration of labour, discovery of new natural resources and improved competition policy. These factors are illustrated in Figure 15.2, where Yf denotes the full employment level of output, indicating the economy is producing at full capacity (operating on its production possibility frontier).

Figure 15.2

Figure 15.3

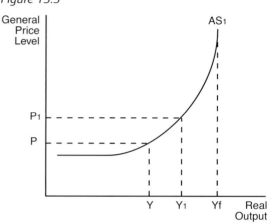

Keynesian aggregate supply (AS)

Keynesian economists dispute the assumption made by classical economists that the prices of factors of production adjust in the long run to bring about full employment of all resources. For example, Keynesians believe that there may be downwards **sticky wages** so that even if there is mass unemployment wages might not fall in the way that would be necessary to encourage firms to hire the unemployed workers.

For this reason, there is a single aggregate supply (AS) curve in Keynesian economics, without the short and long run distinction made by classical economists (as shown in Figure 15.3).

The AS curve is elastic (flat) at low levels of output, because there is substantial spare capacity in the economy. Output can expand quickly without a rise in the price level.

As the economy moves closer to full employment of the factors of production the AS curve becomes more inelastic. Firms start to experience supply bottlenecks and there are shortages of raw materials and labour. This means that firms' costs of production start to rise and, in order to maintain their profit margins, they cannot raise production without increasing their prices.

Eventually when all the factors are fully employed (at Yf in Figure 15.3) it is impossible for firms to produce any extra output and the AS curve becomes completely inelastic. At this point, the economy is operating on its production possibility frontier, at its productive capacity, determined by the quantity and quality of factors of production available.

Macro-economic equilibrium

Macroeconomic equilibrium is achieved when aggregate supply is equal to aggregate demand. The equilibrium is disturbed if one of the curves shifts.

Shifts of the AD curve tend to produce trade-offs with regard to the four main economic indicators. For example, an increase of AD is likely to increase real output and reduce unemployment because of a higher derived demand for labour. However, it will create inflationary pressure, especially if there is only a small output gap. The current account of the balance of payments may deteriorate as higher prices reduce competitiveness and higher demand leads to the 'sucking in' of imports.

On the other hand, shifts of AS tend to improve or worsen all four main economic indicators simultaneously. An increase in the economy's capacity, for instance, allows higher growth (generating employment) and relieves inflationary pressure. Improved competitiveness and available capacity to serve the export market are likely to improve the current account of the balance of payments.

Shifts of AD produce trade-offs

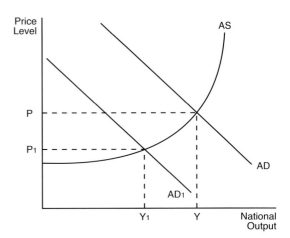

When AD increases:

- Increased output and reduced unemployment.

But

- Inflationary pressure and deterioration of the current account of the balance of payments.

When AD falls:

- Reduced inflationary pressure and improved current account of balance of payments.

But

- Lower output and higher unemployment.

Shifts of AS may move all four main indicators in the same direction

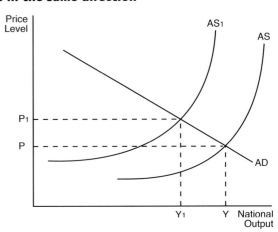

- Potential simultaneous improvement in all four main macroeconomic indicators.

- Potential simultaneous deterioration in all four main macroeconomic indicators.

Here, we are using the Keynesian version of the AS curve to illustrate changes in macroeconomic equilibrium, a convention that is followed later in the book too. However, a classical SRAS curve could have been used with the same effects on the four main economic indicators.

Paper 2: Measuring the macroeconomy → **How the macroeconomy works** → Macroeconomic performance → Macroeconomic policy tools

Consumption, saving and investment

Consumer spending

Consumer spending is also known as **household final consumption expenditure**. It includes **personal expenditure** on **durable and non-durable goods** as well as on **services**. Excluded are all business expenditure and expenses, interest payments and spending on dwellings.

Consumers purchase goods and services for the **direct satisfaction** of individual or collective needs, and expenditure on goods and services in the UK accounts for over **60% of GDP**. A change in consumer expenditure will, therefore, have a much greater impact on GDP than a similar variation in another component of aggregate demand.

Factors affecting consumption

1. Real disposable income

Consumption is likely to increase when real disposable income increases. Real income is money income adjusted for inflation, while disposable income means income after direct taxes and benefits.

Opinions differ as to the strength of the relationship between real disposable income and consumption. Keynes argued that the relationship was strong. Indeed, the **Keynesian consumption function** shows a linear relationship between income and consumption. It is expressed as:

$C = a + bYd$

Where Yd is disposable income and 'b' is the **marginal propensity to consume**, the proportion of each additional pound of income that is spent. It is calculated as $\Delta C/\Delta Yd$ where Δ denotes 'change in'. The marginal propensity to consume is also the gradient of the Keynesian consumption function. Even if disposable income were zero, it is assumed that there would be some consumption financed by running down savings (dissaving). This is seen as 'a' in the function. The Keynesian consumption function is shown in Figure 16.1

Figure 16.1

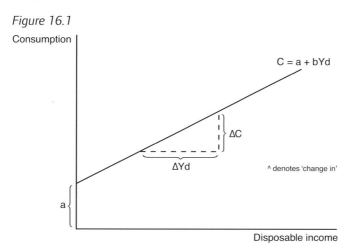

Keynes's view was questioned by Friedman. He suggested that increases in real disposable income only influence consumption if they are believed to be permanent (the **permanent income hypothesis**). Suppose a government cuts taxes prior to a general election. This increases real disposable income but, according to Friedman, may not influence consumption. If consumers perceive this to be only a temporary reduction in their tax burden, purely to boost the government's popularity, then consumption will remain unchanged.

If the Bank of England raises interest rates there is likely to be a fall in demand for consumer durables purchased on credit.

2. Interest rates

Most students can identify that a **rise in interest rates** will **reduce consumer expenditure**, but few can accurately explain precisely how this occurs. If the Bank of England announces a rise in interest rates there is likely to be:

- a **rise in saving**. This is because the **opportunity cost of spending has increased**. If consumers carry on spending they will forego more interest. As a result, saving will probably increase as individuals postpone current consumption in favour of spending in future time periods.

- a **fall in demand** for **consumer durables purchased on credit**. This is because **loan repayments**, on items such as TVs, fridges, cars and holidays, **will increase**.

- a fall in '**discretionary incomes**'. A rise in interest rates will increase **mortgage and other loan repayments**. Effectively, this means that consumers are left with less money in their pockets at the end of each month and consumer expenditure will fall.

All these factors should combine to **reduce the demand for assets** such as housing and shares. If the value of assets falls, consumers' wealth will diminish and, as a result, they may cut back on their spending.

3. Unemployment

A rise in the level of unemployment, or the increased threat of being made jobless, may encourage workers to hold higher **precautionary savings**, which will reduce current consumption. Conversely, a fall in unemployment boosts **consumer confidence** and increases spending.

These effects are also reinforced by the fact that changes in **unemployment** influence the **wages and salaries** earned by those in employment. When the demand for labour increases and unemployment falls, the growth of wages and earnings accelerates. This will boost the spending power of people in work and increase consumer expenditure. Rising unemployment in a recession causes a slowdown in income growth and encourages consumers to rein in their spending plans.

4. Tax burden

In theory, a **rise in direct taxes**, such as income tax and national insurance contributions, will reduce **real disposable income** and the level of consumption. A **rise in indirect taxes**, such as VAT, will directly **increase the prices** of goods and services. Consumers are, therefore, likely to cut back expenditure on those products that are affected by the tax, which reduces consumer expenditure.

A tax change may not always have the effect that an economist expects. A **direct tax cut** may not increase consumer expenditure if it is all saved. This may occur if a consumer is uncertain about the future or believes that a tax cut is transitory. Remember, if a tax cut is perceived to be temporary then it may not increase **permanent income** or consumption.

5. Population

The **age structure** of the population has an impact on household consumption. Many economists believe that consumer spending in future years may be limited by the rising number of 30-50 year olds and pensioners in the population. This can be explained by the **life cycle hypothesis**.

This hypothesis is based on the idea that the level of spending relative to income depends on where the consumer is in their **life cycle**. It suggests that consumers attempt to even out consumption over their lifetime and, as a result, will borrow and save at different ages.

- In the 18-30 age range, consumers will spend more than their current income. They undertake a large number of credit financed purchases; especially relating to housing.

- In middle age, consumers spend less than their current income. They repay their mortgage and other loans and increase **savings** for retirement. This traditional view is becoming less typical in modern society as inheritance and changing family structures, in particular divorce, increasingly influence spending behaviour. Both these factors may stimulate consumption in middle age.

- When consumers reach pensionable age they spend more than their current income. This is because their incomes fall quite sharply and they use up savings made in earlier years.

6. Wealth effects

The **wealth effects** of rising real asset values on consumer expenditure are difficult to quantify, but nevertheless important. When the value of **housing** and other assets (**shares**) is rising faster than income, individuals see a rise in their **net worth** (the difference between the value of their assets and liabilities). This increases consumer confidence and causes consumer expenditure to rise.

Rising house prices may also give rise to a phenomenon known as **mortgage equity withdrawal**. As house prices rise, consumers are able to obtain loans secured on the rising values of their properties. These loans can be used to purchase a wide range of goods and services and will boost consumer expenditure.

However, if asset prices fall, consumers can be left with a **net worth problem**. That is, they have liabilities or debts that exceed the value of their assets. To eliminate this problem consumers have to repay debts by saving. Higher saving means that consumer spending will have to fall.

7. Consumer confidence

Consumer confidence is strongly correlated with expenditure. When confidence is falling it is usually a reliable indicator of a fall in the growth of spending. If consumers become more pessimistic they are less likely to commit themselves to a major 'big-ticket' purchase.

Saving

Income is either consumed or saved. **Saving** is defined as the act of foregoing consumption. It is measured by the **personal sector savings ratio**. The formula is **saving divided by disposable income**. The marginal propensity to save is the proportion of disposable income that is saved: MPS = $\Delta S / \Delta Yd$.

Why do individuals save?
- for retirement
- for big ticket items
- for precautionary motives
- for capital gains
- for future generations

Those factors that promote high levels of consumption lead to low levels of saving.

Savings are important economically:

Private saving takes pressure off the taxpayer, for example to provide for people in their old age.

Savings are channelled by financial institutions to borrowers, many of whom wish to borrow to invest. Higher savings result in more funds available for investment.

Investment spending

Investment is defined as spending on assets which are used repeatedly or continuously over a number of years to produce goods and services. Increased investment in capital goods by firms and the government will allow greater production in future time periods.

Fixed Investment – is spending on new machinery, plant, buildings, vehicles, etc. that will be used continuously or repeatedly in a production process. This would include machinery in a factory, computers in an office and aeroplanes belonging to an airline.

Working Capital – is spending on stocks which are held by their producers before they are sold, stocks of raw materials and work in progress. The accumulation of stocks by firms, whether voluntary or involuntary, is counted as investment.

Net investment – is gross investment with capital depreciation subtracted. Capital depreciation relates to the reduction in the value of an asset due to wear and tear. Net investment must be positive for there to be an increase in the capital stock.

Factors affecting investment spending

1. Changes in aggregate demand
Economic growth can lead to investment according to the **accelerator model** which stresses that **investment is demand induced**. When firms have insufficient capacity, they must invest when demand increases, or they will not be able to satisfy the orders they receive. An increase in demand may therefore lead to a significant acceleration in the rate of investment, especially if spare capacity is limited and the economy's output gap (see Chapter 17) is small.

2. Interest rates
Most students know that higher interest rates should have a negative impact on investment. Few, however, can explain accurately why this happens. The reasons are outlined below:

- Many firms raise finance for investment by borrowing from financial institutions. A rise in interest rates will increase the cost of financing such schemes. This means there will be a rise in the cost of investment relative to the yield and, as a result, some investment projects become unprofitable. A firm will only invest if the yield of a project exceeds the cost.

- A rise in the rate of interest increases the **opportunity cost** of using internal funds to finance investment projects. Some marginal investment projects may not take place as firms decide that they can attain a better rate of return by depositing their retained profits in a bank.

- Higher interest rates **reduce** the level of **aggregate demand**. This reduces investment via the **accelerator process**. Higher interest rates are also likely to **reduce business confidence and corporate profitability**. This applies further downward pressure on investment.

3. Profitability

A rise in the level of corporate profitability should have a positive impact on investment levels. A rise in profitability is usually a signal that the **rate of return** on investment projects will increase and hence more investment projects will become profitable. An increase in profits also allows the firm to invest using internal funds, which are usually cheaper than other forms of corporate finance.

4. Business confidence

This has a strong positive impact on investment levels. Levels of confidence are a function of the factors that we have previously discussed.

5. Government policy and regulations

A fall in **corporation tax** will increase the post-tax rate of return on a new investment with the result that more investment projects become viable. **Tax allowances** also influence the extent to which firms can afford to write off depreciating machinery and replace equipment on a regular basis. In general, lower levels of **government regulation** lead to lower costs of production which encourage firms to invest. Some regulations, such as environmental standards, may however lead firms to invest in new machinery in order to comply.

The economic effects of investment

Why do firms invest?

A positive level of net investment implies a rise in the firm's **capital stock** and a long run expansion. The reasons for undertaking an investment project are varied:

● To take advantage of **higher expected profits** from expanding output.

● To generate a **rise in productive capacity** to meet increased demand.

● To **improve efficiency** via technological progress.

● To **exploit economies of scale** (see Chapter 4).

● As part of a **long run process of capital/labour substitution**; perhaps in response to changes in the relative prices of the factors of production. Higher wage costs relative to capital costs could encourage this strategy.

● As a **barrier to entry** – some investment projects give firms significant cost advantages. This may deter potential competitors from entering a market (see Chapter 5 and the section on monopoly).

Changes in investment will have **short-term effects on the demand side** of the economy and more important **long-term effects on the supply side** of the economy.

Demand side effects of investment

Figure 16.2

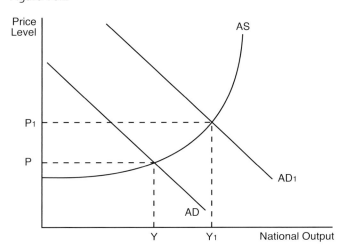

The short-term effects of a rise in investment are examined in Figure 16.2. Investment is a component of aggregate demand and a rise in this variable will shift the aggregate demand curve to the right from AD to AD$_1$. This will result in a rise in national output from Y to Y$_1$, and cause **economic growth** (Chapter 19). The rise in national output will be greater than the change in investment because of the operation of the **multiplier**. There will also be some **demand pull inflation** (see Chapter 19) as the price level has increased from P to P$_1$.

Supply side effects of investment

In the long run, a rise in net investment will increase the **productive capacity** of the economy and, if the new capital embodies new technology, it will also reduce the **costs of production**. A rise in capacity and/or a fall in costs will shift the AS curve to the right. This is illustrated in Figure 16.3. A rise in aggregate supply will cause a rise in national output from Y to Y$_1$ and a fall in the price level from P to P$_1$. This will help the economy to achieve growth without inflation.

Figure 16.3

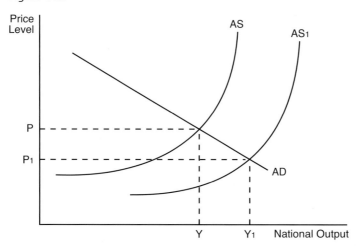

There is a strong positive correlation between investment levels and economic growth. Countries that invest a high proportion of their GDP tend to experience a higher rate of growth. Higher investment should also improve a nation's **international competitiveness**. This will help a country to expand exports of goods and services and compete more effectively against imports from other economies.

New capital machinery is likely to embody new technology. This allows firms who invest heavily to produce goods and provide services of higher quality. Spending which adds to the **stock of capital** can also create new employment in the **capital goods industries**. However, there may be a negative effect on total employment if the main driving force behind investment is to introduce **labour-saving** technology through **capital-labour substitution**.

Chapter

17

Paper 2: Measuring the macroeconomy → How the macroeconomy works →
Macroeconomic performance → Macroeconomic policy tools

Economic growth and living standards

Economic growth

Economic growth is measured as **the increase in real GDP** over a given period of time, usually a year. This figure is expressed as a percentage.

In the long run, the rate of economic growth is determined by the rate at which the economy's capacity (productive potential) increases.

Current (actual or short run) and trend (potential or long run) growth

● **Current growth** is usually caused by an increase in aggregate demand. This draws on the economy's spare capacity, closing the output gap, and bringing unemployed resources into use. Another way of looking at this is that it takes the economy closer to its production possibility frontier. Such growth is not sustainable and will be brought to an end once the economy has no more spare capacity. Further increases in aggregate demand would be purely inflationary once this point is reached.

● **Trend growth** (otherwise known as long run growth or the underlying rate of growth) can be defined in the following ways. (i) It is the long run average growth rate of an economy. (ii) It is the growth rate that the economy can sustain without generating inflationary pressure.

● The trend growth rate of an economy is calculated using data over a substantial period of time, certainly at least one complete business cycle.

● An economy's trend growth rate is determined by the rate at which its capacity grows. A trend growth rate of 2.5%, for example, suggests that on average the capacity of the economy grows at 2.5% a year. Remember that an economy's capacity is a function of the quantity and quality (productivity) of the factors of production (land, labour, capital and enterprise) available.

● The fact that trend growth reflects capacity increases explains why trend growth is sustainable. Capacity increases mean that higher aggregate demand can be accommodated without inflationary pressure.

The economic cycle (the business or trade cycle)

The economy experiences regular cycles, which can be tracked using annual and quarterly movements in real output (GDP). The turning points in the cycle are known as peaks and troughs. Other key terms to be aware of are:

● **Recession.** This refers to falling output and is usually defined as at least two successive quarters of negative growth. (see A-B in Figure 17.1)

● **Recovery.** This is the period between the trough of the business cycle and the next peak. This period is also sometimes known as a boom, but the term 'boom' may be better used to describe a period of very rapid, above-trend growth (see point B onwards in Figure 17.1).

The business cycle shows us how GDP changes over time and therefore shows current growth, which largely reflects changes in aggregate demand. We should also be aware of the supply side, however. Recessions can be caused by supply side factors such as higher oil prices as well as by restricted aggregate demand.

The best fit line drawn through the business cycle shows the trend growth rate of the economy.

Figure 17.1

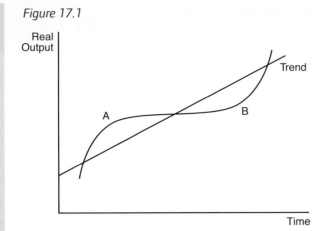

The output gap and the economic cycle

- The **output gap** is the difference between actual and potential real GDP.

- If the economy grows faster than trend for any significant period of time, this suggests aggregate demand is growing faster than capacity. This is likely to reduce unemployment, but may be inflationary as the output gap closes. There may even be a positive output gap, with the economy temporarily operating beyond full capacity (for example, through overtime work).

- Below trend growth suggests that demand is growing more slowly than capacity. The output gap grows and so too does unemployment, but inflationary pressure is reduced.

- If the economy grows at trend, no inflationary pressure is generated and economic stability is enhanced. Once again, trend growth is seen as the sustainable growth rate for the economy.

Figure 17.2

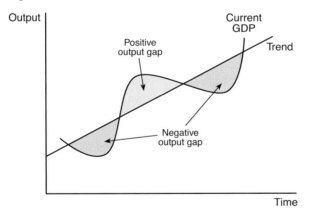

What determines the trend growth rate of the economy?

Given that trend growth is determined by the rate at which economic capacity increases, we need to look at the influences on the quantity and quality of factors of production to find out what determines trend growth.

Economies with high trend growth rates tend to:

- Invest a substantial proportion of their GDP, thus boosting the quantity and quality of their capital stock.

- Devote resources to research and development in order to achieve technological advances (although it is also possible to receive external benefits as a third party gaining from technological advances made by other countries).

- Have high quality education and training systems, raising the productivity of workers.

- Have 'flexible labour markets' with workers willing to adapt to new working practices, thereby enhancing their productivity.

- Benefit from a strong entrepreneurial culture, perhaps supported by a policy framework of low corporate taxes and only light regulation by the government.

- Possess a strong institutional structure. This might imply adequate protection of property rights, including patents for 'intellectual property' such as new ideas. There should also be a strong financial system to provide the finance that firms need in order to invest and innovate.

Advantages and disadvantages of economic growth

Advantages of Economic Growth

1. Higher economic growth should lead to an increase in **living standards** as measured by real GDP per capita.

2. The effects of growth are **cumulative**. If a country grows at 3% per annum, the economy will double in size every 24 years. Growth helps make future investment more affordable.

3. Economic growth should reduce **unemployment**. When output in the economy increases there should be an increase in the demand for labour. This is because labour is a **derived demand**, that is the demand for labour is dependent on the final demand for goods and services. Firms do not demand labour for its own sake.

4. Economic growth will have a positive effect on **government finances**. Economic growth will **increase tax revenues** because as output, employment and incomes rise so will the tax take. Growth will reduce unemployment and, as a result, **expenditure on transfer payments** will fall. These two effects will combine to reduce the budget deficit (see Chapter 22). Alternatively the government could increase spending on areas such as education and health without having to put up taxes and reduce current consumption levels.

5. Rising demand and output encourages further **investment** in new capital machinery via the **accelerator process**. This will boost the productive capacity of the economy in the long run.

Disadvantages of Economic Growth

1. If current growth exceeds trend growth there is the danger of **inflation**. The rise in prices may reduce the **international competitiveness** of the economy.

2. Economic growth will create **negative externalities**, such as increased pollution and congestion, which will damage social welfare. Those affected could experience a fall in living standards.

3. The benefits of **economic growth may not be evenly distributed**. A rise in national output may also be associated with growing inequality in society. Just because there is economic growth, it does not mean that the number of people living **below the poverty line**, i.e. in absolute poverty, will diminish.

4. Faster economic growth might lead to an **over exploitation of scarce finite economic resources** that will limit growth prospects in the future.

The material in the rest of this chapter is required for AS-level by Edexcel and in A-level Year 2 by other exam boards.

National income and living standards

It is important to understand that income and wealth are not the same thing. **Wealth** consists of a **stock of assets**. An economy's assets are the factors of production available to it.

Income is a **flow** derived from the stock of assets that make up wealth. These are factor payments earned by factors of production, which sum to give national income.

Wealthy countries tend to have high incomes because income is derived from the stock of assets that make up wealth, but income and wealth are not the same thing.

It is common to use national income as an indicator of a country's living standards. **GDP per capita** (GDP divided by population) is the most frequently used variable for this purpose. However, it should be noted that GDP per capita figures are only an indication of **material living standards** and tell us nothing about the non-material aspects of quality of life. Even comparing material living standards is difficult.

GDP per capita figures may not give an accurate comparison even of material living standards

Difficulties in using GDP per capita figures to measure material living standards include:

- **The figures take no account of the distribution of income.** The income of a country with a high GDP per capita figure may be concentrated in the hands of a small section of the population, with the rest of the population being poor. This tends to be the case in oil rich countries, for example. In the UK there are significant pockets of poverty, despite our high per capita GDP. The degree of inequality can be examined using the concepts of the **Lorenz curve and Gini coefficient** (see later in this chapter).

- **GDP figures understate national income because they do not include the majority of illegal activity.** However, the UK does now include estimates of the value of trade in illegal drugs and prostitution in its GDP figures.

- **GDP figures understate national income because they do not include the value of non-traded output.** We all produce valuable economic output that we do not trade. If households paid someone else to do all their washing, ironing, cooking, cleaning, decorating and other maintenance currently undertaken on a do-it-yourself basis, this would add hugely to national income. In developing countries, subsistence agriculture (families growing crops for consumption rather than trade) means that GDP figures significantly underestimate income.

- **Price changes can make it difficult to compare GDP per capita over time.** This means that GDP per capita figures should be adjusted for inflation to give real GDP per capita.

- **It is necessary to convert GDP per capita figures into a common currency in order to make international comparisons possible.** The American dollar is often used for this purpose.

- **The choice of the exchange rate for making the converting to a common currency crucially affects the outcome.** Converting the UK GDP per capita at £1 = $1.80 instead of £1 = $1.50 would give a 20% higher per capita income in dollars. The correct exchange rate to use is the **purchasing power parity** (**PPP**) exchange rate, which adjusts for price differentials between countries (PPP exchange rates give the same purchasing power for any given sum of money when it is converted into another currency). The GDP per capita of developing countries tends to be higher when using purchasing power parity rates for conversion than when using market exchange rates. This is because any given sum of money has greater purchasing power in developing countries due to the low price levels there.

- **International comparisons can be difficult due to differences in accounting procedures and accuracy of GDP statistics collected in different countries.**

Non-material aspects of standard of living, including environmental, social, education and health indicators

There is clearly more to having a good standard of living than how many goods and services a society is able to produce and consume. A more complete picture would take account of a variety of other factors. These might include:

● **Environmental indicators** such as air quality, water quality, greenhouse gas emissions, access to green space and areas of outstanding natural beauty, biodiversity (number of different species of plants and wildlife, for example) and so on. A moderate climate is generally thought to be an advantage.

● **Social indicators** such as crime rates, divorce rates and quality of human relationships (although this is very difficult to measure). 'Work-life balance' has become a particular issue in developed nations. This links to the length of the average working week and by implication to the amount of leisure time enjoyed.

● **Educational indicators** such as literacy and numeracy rates, percentage of the relevant age group enrolled in primary, secondary and higher education and so on. The rate of primary school enrolment is particularly important in developing countries.

● **Health indicators** such as life expectancy and infant mortality rates and indicators relating to particular illnesses such as heart disease (heart disease is a particular concern in richer, developed nations). The incidence of depression and stress-related illnesses also receives particular attention in developed nations.

● **Political freedoms** such as the right to vote, free speech and so on.

National happiness and UK well-being

There is a growing interest in trying to measure non-material aspects of the standard of living and indeed to measure 'national happiness'. This is problematic because happiness is so subjective, although it is possible to conduct surveys asking people to rate their happiness on a scale of, say, 1 to 10.

It is possible to argue that enjoying a high national income often comes at the expense of non-material aspects of quality of living and happiness. High levels of economic activity may contribute to environmental damage through negative externalities such as **resource depletion** (fewer resources available in the future, especially non-renewables such as fossil fuel) and **resource degradation** (polluted rivers are less useful, for example). High material living standards may be achieved through long working hours, contributing to stress related illnesses.

The UK has led the way in developing measures of living standards and now publishes a host of statistics measuring both material and non-material aspects. These include survey data on satisfaction with life overall, happiness, satisfaction with social life and so on.

Measuring inequality: the Lorenz curve and the Gini coefficient

Figure 17.3

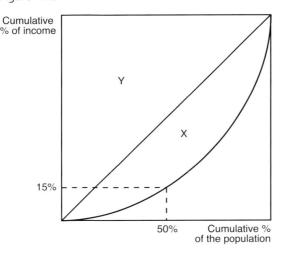

The degree of inequality in an economy can be examined by looking at the **Lorenz Curve**. In Figure 17.3, the cumulative percentage of income is plotted along the y-axis and the cumulative percentage of the population is plotted along the x-axis. A diagonal 45° line represents complete equality in income distribution because the poorest 10% of the population receive 10% of the income, while the richest 10% also only receive 10% of the income.

The further the curve bows away from 45°, the greater the level of inequality. In this diagram there is significant inequality as the poorest 50% of the population only earn 15% of total income. There is a numerical measure of inequality derived from the Lorenz Curve called the **Gini Coefficient**.

This is calculated by dividing area X by area Y in the diagram. Area X lies between the Lorenz Curve and the 45° line while Y is the total area above the 45° line. If the Gini coefficient is **zero** then there is complete **equality** and if it is one there is **total inequality** (one person enjoys all the income). It is easy to remember that the greater the Gini Coefficient the more the inequality.

The Human Development Index (HDI)

The **Human Development Index** (**HDI**) is an indicator of economic development published by the United Nations. It is an indicator composed of three variables:

- **Gross Domestic Product per capita**, measured in US dollars, using purchasing power parity exchange rates for conversions.

- **Life expectancy** in years.

- The **adult literacy** rate.

The HDI gives a better picture of a country's development and living standards than using GDP per capita alone. It is possible for countries to be ranked very differently in an 'HDI league table' compared to one for GDP. Oil rich nations, for example, tend to do well in GDP terms but relatively badly on HDI.

However, the HDI is far from being a complete measure of development. There are many factors discussed in the preceding sub-sections that it does not include. Countries could fare well in HDI terms, but still have poor living standards in many other respects. It would be possible, for instance, for a country with a high HDI figure to have very low environmental standards and not offer political freedoms to its citizens.

Other measures of development

For developing countries, economists may pay particular attention to indicators that seem less relevant in richer, developed economies. Such indicators include:

- The percentage of adult male labour in agriculture. As an economy develops, workers tend to move out of the primary sector of the economy and into the secondary and tertiary sectors.

- Primary and secondary school enrolment figures have implications for literacy, numeracy and other valuable skills and make a significant difference to the future productive capacity of the economy.

- Access to clean water is particularly important in societies where not all citizens have their basic economic needs met and absolute poverty is a concern.

- Energy consumption per capita, which tends to increase as countries become more economically developed.

- Access to mobile phones per thousand of the population. Communication links are valuable both for social reasons and for the organisation of economic activity.

Chapter

18

Paper 2: Measuring the macroeconomy → How the macroeconomy works →
Macroeconomic performance → Macroeconomic policy tools

Unemployment

Definition of unemployment

Unemployment consists of those of a working age who are actively seeking employment but do not have a job.

Chapter 13 gives details on how unemployment is measured.

Causes of unemployment and policy to reduce it

Unemployment has a number of different causes. It can result from a lack of demand (demand deficient unemployment) or various problems on the supply side of the economy (real-wage unemployment, frictional unemployment and structural unemployment).

The policies appropriate to tackling unemployment depend crucially on what has caused the unemployment in the first place.

Demand deficient unemployment

Demand deficient unemployment is associated with an **economic recession**. Labour is a **derived demand** – it is not demanded for its own sake, but because of the output that it produces. A fall in the level of output will cause a drop in the demand for labour at each wage level. As aggregate demand drops, firms will lay-off workers to reduce their costs and protect profits.

Figure 18.1

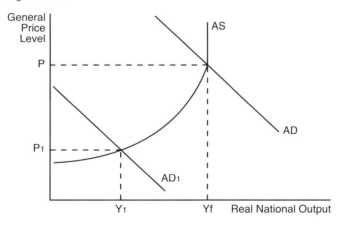

In Figure 18.1, the equilibrium level of national output (Y₁) lies below the full employment level of national output (Yf). This means that there is insufficient aggregate demand for all workers to obtain employment. The current level of demand (AD₁) lies below the level required for full employment (AD).

Although demand deficient unemployment is usually associated with economic recessions it can also exist in the long run when the economy has an **output gap**. This occurs when actual output lies below potential output.

Policies for demand deficient unemployment

The usual government response is to raise aggregate demand. This can be achieved by utilising a variety of policy instruments.

● **Increase Government Expenditure** – this will boost aggregate demand because it is one of its components. The change in national output will be greater than the change in government expenditure because of the operation of the **multiplier**. The larger the value of the multiplier the greater the effect on national output. If the government raises expenditure on infrastructure, or training, it will also boost the productive potential of the economy and shift the AS curve to the right.

● **Reduce Taxation** – lower income taxes will increases consumers' real disposable incomes and boost consumer expenditure.

● **Lower interest rates** – will encourage borrowing, reduce saving and increase consumers' real discretionary incomes. This should boost consumer expenditure and the level of aggregate demand. A drop in interest rates may also encourage firms to invest, as the cost of investment will fall.

● **Depreciate the pound** – this should lead to a rise in export orders for UK firms and to a fall in imports. This is because a fall in the value of the currency will reduce the price of exports and increase the cost of imports.

Remember the effects of monetary and fiscal policy are not instantaneous. It will take some time for the full effect of these policies to impact on output and employment.

Real wage unemployment

Real wage unemployment is a form of **disequilibrium unemployment** that occurs when **real wages** are forced above **the market clearing level**. Traditionally, **trade unions** and **minimum wage legislation** have been seen as the main cause of this type of unemployment.

Suppose that having initially been in equilibrium where the demand for labour was equal to the supply of labour, a minimum wage W_1 is set above the market clearing wage W. The effects of such an action are illustrated in Figure 18.2.

Figure 18.2

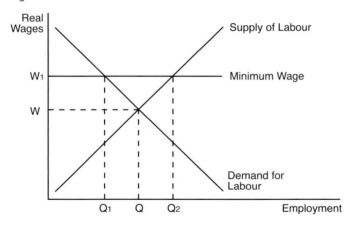

At the new minimum wage W_1, the **demand for labour** has contracted from Q to Q_1 while the supply of labour has expanded from Q to Q_2. Firms will tend to employ fewer workers when the **marginal cost** of employing them increases. At the same time, more workers will be willing to take jobs at higher wage rates.

At real wage W_1, there is an **excess supply of labour**. The supply of labour now exceeds the demand for labour and we have disequilibrium unemployment equal to Q_1-Q_2.

We are assuming that a rise in real wages does not cause a rise in productivity or consumer expenditure. If productivity, and/or consumption, did increase then the demand for labour would shift to the right and the rise in unemployment would be far smaller.

Policies to reduce real wage unemployment

Most prescriptions for reducing real wage unemployment centre around the idea of making each labour market more **flexible**, so that pay conditions become more adaptable to changing demand and supply conditions. Real wages should rise when demand, output and employment are rising, but they may need to fall if an industry experiences a recession which puts jobs at threat. Flexible labour markets involve working practices such as part-time and temporary contracts and shift work, as well as an absence of union power.

The national minimum wage (NMW) could be seen as a source of real wage employment. Supporters of flexible labour markets would argue for the abolition of minimum wages.

Frictional unemployment

This type of unemployment reflects **job turnover** in the labour market. Even when there are vacancies it takes people time to **search** and find a new job. During this period of time workers will remain frictionally unemployed.

Policies for frictional unemployment

● **Reduce Job Seeker's Allowance** (formerly unemployment benefit) – The job seeker has to show that he/she is **actively seeking work** and if they are unable to prove this at fortnightly interviews they lose their benefit. This measure was introduced to reduce the level of frictional unemployment. However, if the government reduced the level of the benefit, or limited the duration of a claim, search times between jobs could be reduced even further. This is because workers would have to take a job more quickly before their financial situations deteriorated. Some economists argue that if the unemployed were financially worse off they would not be able to search for work effectively. For example, they may not be able to afford to travel to interviews or telephone potential employers.

● **Direct tax cuts** – the government could reduce direct taxes for the low paid to increase the post tax wage and, therefore, encourage them to find work more quickly. Most analysts believe that tax cuts on their own are insufficient to reduce frictional unemployment. The benefit system needs to be reformed to eliminate the **unemployment trap** – this is a situation where someone is financially better off not working.

● **Improve job information** – facilities provided by job centres, private agencies, newspapers and the Internet. The development of the Job Centre Plus programme, which provides intensive support and advice for job seekers, is one way to help workers obtain employment more quickly.

Structural unemployment

Structural unemployment occurs when there is a mismatch between the characteristics of the unemployed and the characteristics needed in order to fill the vacancies in an economy.

Structural unemployment is caused by immobility of labour:

● **Occupational immobility** is associated with a lack of transferable skills, preventing workers from moving from one job to another.

● **Geographical immobility** prevents workers moving from one area to another in order to fill vacancies.

Structural unemployment is often centred on certain **regions** due to the long term decline of traditional manufacturing industries, such as coal, steel, textiles and shipbuilding. Employment in these sectors contracts due to intense overseas competition and the development of new technology.

Policies for the structural problem

There are a number of different approaches that can be adopted to help alleviate structural unemployment. These are sometimes known as **active labour market policies**.

● **Regional policy** – gives grants and tax breaks to encourage firms to locate in areas of high structural unemployment. This, however, does not solve the problem of **occupational immobility**. Regional policy often demands extra retraining schemes in order to give workers the relevant skills to allow them to take up new jobs.

- **Investment in worker training and skills** – The problem of **occupational immobility** can be reduced if learners are able to learn new skills which are relevant to the modern labour market. They may then be able to fill existing job vacancies in areas of skill shortages, for example. It is particularly useful to train workers in **transferable skills** which can be used in many different jobs, while there is also an increased emphasis on **vocational training** for particular jobs where there is a high demand for labour.

- **Improving geographical mobility** – The government could provide grants or low cost housing to encourage workers to move from areas of high unemployment to regions where there are jobs. The problem with this policy is that people are inherently immobile because they are often bound by family and social ties.

- **The market solution** – one approach is simply to leave the problem of structural unemployment to the market. High unemployment will **drive down wages** and **new firms will be attracted into a region** to take advantage of the low costs of production. In this way the problem will eventually solve itself, but the **social deprivation created** in the short term may be considerable. Some commentators argue that intervention to solve structural unemployment slows the natural reallocation of resources to high growth areas and only makes the problem worse.

Causes of unemployment: summary

Demand or supply side?	Type	Cause
Demand	Demand deficient	A lack of derived demand for labour, creating an output gap. Typically occurring during recession.
Supply	Real wage	A real wage above the equilibrium in the labour market, generating an excess supply of labour.
Supply	Frictional	Search periods between jobs, possibly reflecting a lack of information about vacancies or generous unemployment benefits.
Supply	Structural	Mismatch caused by occupational and geographical immobility of labour.

The costs of unemployment

The costs of high levels of unemployment include:

- **Lost output** – unemployment causes a waste of scarce economic resources and reduces the growth potential of the economy. An economy with unemployment is producing inside its **production possibility frontier** (see Chapter 1). The hours that the unemployed do not work can never be recovered.

- **Impact on government expenditure, taxation and the budget deficit** – an increase in unemployment results in higher benefit payments and lower tax revenues. When individuals are unemployed, not only do they receive benefits but they pay no income tax. Because they are spending less, they contribute less to the government in indirect taxes. This rise in government spending, along with the fall in tax revenues, may result in a budget deficit (see Chapter 24).

- **Unemployment wastes some of the resources used in training workers.** Furthermore, workers who are unemployed for long periods become **de-skilled** as their skills become increasingly dated in a rapidly changing job market. This reduces their chances of gaining employment in the future, which in turn increases the burden on the government and the taxpayer.

Workers who are unemployed for long periods become de-skilled as their skills become increasingly dated in a rapidly changing job market

● **Rising unemployment is linked to social and economic deprivation** – there is some relationship with crime and with social dislocation (increased divorce, worsening health and lower life expectancy). Areas of high unemployment will see falls in real incomes and an increase in income inequality.

The growing labour supply and unemployment

The supply of those willing and available to work can increase for a number of reasons. Factors increasing the labour force in the UK include greater **female participation** in the labour market and **later retirement**. **Inwards migration** also adds to the labour supply. In theory, a greater number of available workers could increase unemployment if there were the same number of jobs. However, many of those joining the labour force offer skills which are in short supply and fill what would otherwise be persistent vacancies. Economic theory also suggests that increases in the labour supply may put downward pressure on wages and create extensions of labour demand, generating more jobs.

Chapter

19

Paper 2: Measuring the macroeconomy → How the macroeconomy works →
Macroeconomic performance → Macroeconomic policy tools

Inflation and deflation

Definition:

Inflation

Inflation is a sustained increase in the general price level over a period of time causing a fall in the purchasing power of money. Inflation can be measured via the retail price index (RPI) or consumer price index (CPI). Further details can be found in Chapter 13.

Deflation

Deflation is a sustained fall in the general price level over a period of time, causing an increase in the purchasing power of money

Disinflation

Disinflation is a fall in the rate of inflation in an economy.

Hyperinflation

Hyperinflation occurs when the rate of inflation is very high and unpredictable, sufficiently so to disrupt the functions of money. When the rate of inflation is very high, for example, people may be reluctant to accept money in payment for goods and services (as a medium of exchange) because the value of the money will be eroded so quickly by inflation.

Causes of inflation

Demand pull inflation occurs when **total demand for goods and services exceeds total supply**. This type of inflation happens when there has been **excessive growth in aggregate demand** or when **current growth exceeds trend growth**.

**Demand pull
inflation**

Figure 19.1

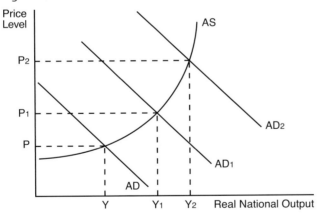

- At low levels of output when there is plenty of **spare productive capacity** (a substantial output gap) firms can easily expand output to meet increases in demand, resulting in a relatively elastic AS curve (see the shift from AD to AD₁, giving only moderate inflation of P to P₁).

- However, as the economy **approaches full capacity** and the output gap closes, labour and raw material shortages mean that it becomes more difficult for firms to expand production without pushing up their prices (see the shift from AD₁ to AD₂, giving more substantial inflation from P₁ to P₂).

- At the same time, many firms will choose to widen their **profit margins**. As a result, prices will rise sharply.

- It is likely that, as employment in the economy grows, demand for goods and services will become more inelastic. This will allow firms to pass on large price increases without any significant fall in demand.

Growth of the **money supply** is a particular cause of demand-pull inflation. In simple terms, the higher the money supply the more spending is possible. A situation of "too much money chasing too few goods" can arise, with excess demand causing inflation. Monetarist economists believe that growth of the money supply is as the root of all inflation.

The Fisher Equation, **MV = PT**, is true by definition (where M is the money supply, V the velocity of circulation – the number of times each pound of the money supply is spent each time period, P the general price level and T the number of transactions per time period). The left hand side of the equation shows expenditure and the right hand side output, which are identical. Monetarist economists believe that the velocity of circulation is broadly constant. If the money supply grows more quickly than the transactions in the economy (which grow as GDP grows) then inflation is inevitable.

Cost push inflation

This occurs when firms increase prices to maintain or protect profit margins after experiencing a rise in costs. The main causes are:

● Growth in **unit labour costs** – this occurs when average wages grow faster than productivity.

● Rising **input costs** – such as oil, raw materials and components.

● Increases in **indirect taxes** – VAT and excise duties are paid by producers and will, therefore, increase their costs.

● **Higher import prices** – a depreciation in the currency or a rise in world inflation rates will force up import prices.

Figure 19.2

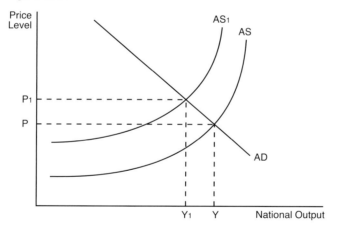

The effects of a rise in costs is illustrated in Figure 19.2.

● An increase in **input costs** will mean that firms can produce less at each and every price level and, as a result, the **aggregate supply curve will shift to the left** from AS to AS1.

● At the new equilibrium level of national output, the economy is producing a lower level of output (Y1) at a higher price level (P1). Higher cost push inflation therefore causes a contraction in real output as well as a higher price level.

● However, increases in the costs of firms do not always feed through to inflation. Firms may choose to absorb the increase in costs and accept reduced profit margins on each unit sold, especially when the consumer is very sensitive to price increases as may be the case during and immediately after a recession.

Stagflation	Figure 19.2 suggests that substantial cost increases **could** give rise to an unpleasant combination of economic circumstances. Rapidly rising oil prices, for example, could lead to a stagnating economy (**negative or sluggish growth with rising unemployment**) combined with high inflation. This is known as **stagflation**.
Policies to control inflation	A summary of policies that could be used to control inflation is given here. More detail on the main policy tools available for the government to influence the economy (fiscal, monetary and supply side policies) is given in Chapters 22 to 24.

Policies to control inflation – summary

Demand side (short term) or supply side (long term)?	Policy type	Policy options
Demand side	Fiscal policy	Cut government spending or raise taxes in order to reduce consumption and restrict AD.
Demand side	Monetary policy	Raise interest rates in order to reduce consumption and investment, restricting AD.
		Engineer an exchange rate appreciation, reducing net exports (X-M) and restricting AD. This would also limit cost push by reducing the price of imported raw materials.
Supply side	Supply side policies	Market based reforms to increase productivity and create incentives to boost the trend growth rate of the economy.

Costs and effects of inflation	The costs and effects of inflation include:

1. Inflation distorts the operation of the price mechanism and can result in an **inefficient allocation of resources**. When inflation is volatile, consumers and firms are unlikely to have sufficient information on relative price levels to make informed choices about which products to purchase and supply.

2. **Effect on UK competitiveness** – if the UK has higher inflation than the rest of the world it will lose competitiveness in the international market. This assumes a given exchange rate. This rise in relative inflation leads to a fall in the world share of UK exports and a rise in import penetration. See Chapter 20 on the current account of the balance of payments. Ultimately, this will lead to a fall in the rate of economic growth and the level of employment.

3. **The problems of a wage-price spiral** – price rises can lead to higher wage demands as workers try to maintain their standard of living. This increases firms' costs and, in an effort to maintain their profit margins, they increase prices. The process could start all over again and inflation may get out of control. Higher inflation causes an upward shift in **inflationary expectations** that are then incorporated into wage bargaining. It can take some time for these expectations to be controlled.

4. **Reduction in the real value of savings** – especially if real interest rates (interest rates – inflation) are negative. This means the rate of interest does not fully compensate for the increase in the general price level. In contrast, **borrowers** see the **real value of their debt diminish**. Inflation, therefore, favours borrowers at the expense of savers.

5. **Consumers and businesses on fixed incomes will lose out.** This may include some with fixed private pensions such that inflation reduces the real value of their income year-on-year. The value of

the state pension is protected from such loss of value as it goes up in April each year by the highest of: (i) Average wage growth; (ii) CPI inflation in the previous September; (iii) 2.5%.

6. Inflation usually leads to **higher interest rates**, which will reduce economic growth and employment.

7. **Disruption of business planning** – high and volatile inflation creates uncertainty about the future. This makes planning and budgeting difficult as firms become unsure about what will happen to their costs. This could have a detrimental effect on investment in the economy. For example, if inflation is high and volatile, firms may demand a higher rate of return on investment projects before they will go ahead with the capital spending. These **hurdle rates** may cause projects to be cancelled or postponed until economic conditions improve. A low rate of capital investment clearly damages the productive potential of the economy and may reduce productivity growth.

8. Cost inflation usually leads to a slower growth of **profits** and this is likely to reduce the level of investment in the economy.

9. **Shoe leather costs** – when prices are unstable there will be an increase in search times to discover more about prices. Inflation increases the opportunity cost of holding money, so people make more visits to their banks and building societies (wearing out their shoe leather!).

10. **Menu costs** – are the extra costs to firms of changing price information.

Should there be a target rate of inflation?

There is a debate about whether having a target rate is helpful. On the one hand it may give policy **credibility**, reducing expectations of inflation, wage demands and therefore reducing inflation itself. On the other hand, governments may have to **sacrifice economic growth** to meet the target.

Causes of deflation

Persistent falls in the general price level can be caused by a **severe lack of demand** in an economy, for example during a very serious recession or a period of enforced **government austerity** (cuts in government spending). Deflation can also occur from the **supply side**, for example during a period of falling raw material costs such as lower oil prices, or as a result of significant technological advances.

The consequences of deflation

Deflation is generally considered to be economically undesirable the main reasons for this are:

● It may encourage **deferred spending**. If consumers believe that cars will be cheaper in the future, for example, they are unlikely to buy one now. The more spending is deferred, the lower aggregate demand and the lower GDP, with effects such as higher unemployment. This makes further deflation likely and the economy can become caught in a downward spiral. This may be so serious that any government attempts to stimulate spending in the economy are ineffective.

● **Deflation increases the real value of debts.** This makes debt more difficult to repay and increases the likelihood of debt default. Banks who suffer from bad debt (unpaid debts) are less able to lend to firms who wish to borrow for investment. This can reinforce the stagnation of the economy.

However, it is sometimes argued that while demand side deflation is **malevolent** (bad), supply side deflation can be more beneficial. Technological advances leading to lower prices may encourage consumers to spend, for example.

Chapter

20

Paper 2: Measuring the macroeconomy → How the macroeconomy works →
Macroeconomic performance → **International trade** → Macroeconomic policy tools

The current account of the balance of payments

The current account of the balance of payments

The current account primarily measures net trade in goods and services. For further details, see Chapter 13, which also includes details of the other sections of the balance of payments accounts.

The current account and the economic cycle

The current account tends to **deteriorate** during the recovery phase of the business cycle and deteriorate to an even greater extent if this **recovery** becomes a **boom**. This is because growing income generates growing demand for goods and services. Inevitably this means growing demand for imports, both from consumers and firms. This is sometimes known as 'sucking in' imports.

The extent to which imports rise when incomes grow is measured by the **income elasticity of demand for imports**. This examines the responsiveness of the demand for imports to a change in the income of consumers. The income elasticity of demand for imports tends to rise when the economy is nearing full capacity, as it is increasingly difficult for demand to be met from domestic production.

While the current account deteriorates when income grows, it is likely to improve if incomes fall, resulting in lower demand for imports. Current account deficits can therefore be **cyclical**. A deficit that persists regardless of the stage of the economic cycle is known as a **structural deficit**.

Are current account deficits always a bad thing?

A common misconception is that current account deficits are always bad for the economy. This is not necessarily true. In the short term, if a country is importing a high volume of goods and services then this can boost **living standards**. It allows consumers to buy a higher level of **consumer durables** and other items. A cyclical current account deficit is generally not a concern.

However, in the long term a current account deficit may be a symptom of a weakening domestic economy and a **lack of international competitiveness**. It could be a sign of low levels of productivity and high domestic production costs, for example. If imports continue to rise, this will threaten domestic employment and incomes and **living standards may fall**.

For this reason, governments prefer to avoid substantial and persistent current account deficits (structural deficits).

Causes of a current account deficit

Some of the more common causes of a current account deficit are:

- **Growing income** – In recoveries and especially booms, when consumption and investment expenditure tend to rise, it is inevitable that some of this increased spending will leave the country as consumers and firms purchase imports. Other things being equal, this will cause the **current account balance to deteriorate**. The higher the income elasticity of demand for imports, the greater the increase in imports will be.

- **Lack of productive capacity of domestic firms** – If home producers have insufficient capacity to meet rising demand from consumers then imports of goods and services will come into the country to satisfy this excess demand. As a result, the current account will worsen.

- **Poor price and non price competitiveness** – Competitiveness can be measured by cost levels and domestic prices relative to international competitors, but non price factors are also important. These include quality, design, reliability and after-sales service. Inflation is a key determinant of international competitiveness. If the UK has higher inflation than the rest of the world has, it will lose competitiveness in international markets. Assuming that the quality of goods and services and the exchange rate remain unchanged, the rise in relative inflation will reduce UK exports and increase import penetration, and result in a deterioration of the current account.

- **Increased competition from other nations** – The advantages that countries have in producing certain goods and services can change over time, as technology alters and other countries exploit their economic resources and develop competing industries. The UK manufacturing sector, for example, has suffered over the last 25 years from the emergence of low cost production in newly industrialised countries.

- **An over-valued exchange rate** – Some economists believe that current account deficits stem from the exchange rate being at too high a level. A high exchange rate causes export prices to be higher in foreign markets whilst imports become relatively cheaper. Other things being equal, this will cause imports to rise, exports to fall and the current account balance to worsen.

- **Falling surplus in an important mineral resource** – Some countries rely heavily on the export of specific primary commodities whose prices on international markets might be highly volatile. A fall in price when demand from purchasers is inelastic can cause a sharp fall in total export revenues and a sudden deterioration in a country's current account.

Policies to reduce a current account deficit: expenditure reducing policies

Expenditure reducing policies aim to **reduce the spending of consumers and firms** so that the demand for imports falls. The following policies could be introduced:

- **Higher income taxes** will reduce real disposable incomes and should lead to a fall in expenditure on imports.

- **Higher interest rates** will discourage borrowing, increase saving and reduce consumers' real 'effective' disposable incomes. This should lead to a fall in consumer spending and a reduction in the level of imports.

The problem will these policies is that they only provide a **short term solution** and do not tackle the underlying causes of persistent account deficits (such as a lack of competitiveness). They also reduce aggregate demand and this will result in **lower economic growth and higher unemployment**.

Policies to reduce a current account deficit: expenditure switching policies

Expenditure switching policies attempt to encourage consumers to **switch** their demand away from imports and towards the output of domestic firms. This occurs if the price of imports can be raised, or if the price of UK products can be lowered. This change in relative prices should then cause a change in spending patterns in favour of output produced within the domestic economy. Expenditure switching policies include:

- A **devaluation** or **depreciation** of the exchange rate will reduce the price of exports and increase the price of imports. This policy will be most effective if the price elasticities of demand are high for both exports and imports, maximising the response of consumers and firms to the change in relative prices. This is more likely to be the case in the long run than in the short run, as it is more likely that spending patterns will adapt after a greater period of time has elapsed. (See Chapter 21 for more detail on this policy.)

- The introduction of **tariffs** (a tax on imports) or other import controls will reduce imports (see Chapter 21). They will however raise prices for domestic consumers and may not be compatible with membership of organisations such as the EU and the World Trade Organisation.

- **Supply side policies** to improve **competitiveness**. The aim is to reduce unit costs of domestic firms, for example by encouraging greater investment and improved labour productivity. Measures to encourage innovation would also help improve competitiveness. Such policies take time to be effective, but address the underlying causes of persistent deficits. Economists would tend to look favourably at this way of switching expenditure towards domestically produced output.

Chapter

21

Paper 2: Measuring the macroeconomy → How the macroeconomy works →
Macroeconomic performance → **International trade** → Macroeconomic policy tools

International trade and exchange rates

This chapter is primarily aimed at students following the OCR AS-level specification. AQA and Edexcel students will encounter this material in A-level Year 2.

Why do countries trade with each other?

International trade is an extension of the basic economic concepts of **specialisation and exchange**. Recall from Chapter 1 that self-sufficiency would imply low living standards and that specialisation and then exchange (trade) of the goods and services produced is necessary to **escape self sufficiency**.

This applies to countries just as it does to individuals. A country with a **closed economy**, and no trade with other countries, can only consume the items that it produces domestically. Countries with economies that are **open to trade** tend to enjoy higher living standards. The rapid growth of living standards in China since it began to participate fully in the international economy provides strong evidence for this.

In short, trade is the necessary consequence of an **international division of labour** with countries specialising in the products that they can produce most efficiently relative to other nations.

A general summary of the benefits of international trade might read as follows:

1. Trade can lead to an improvement in overall **economic welfare** if countries **specialise** in the products that they produce most efficiently in comparison to other nations.

2. There are some goods that we cannot produce in this country because of inappropriate resources and the wrong climate. Good examples include bananas, bauxite and gold. We need to **export** goods to fund **imports** of these items.

3. Trade allows firms to exploit **economies of scale** by operating in much larger markets. Economies of scale lead to **lower average costs** of production and can be passed onto consumers in the form of **lower prices**. The UK's membership of the EU gives British firms access to an enormous market.

4. **International competition** stimulates **higher productive efficiency**. Lower average costs should feed through to **lower prices** in the shops benefiting consumers. Overseas competition can also stop domestic monopolies from exploiting their position.

5. Trade enhances **consumer choice**. When a British consumer purchases a new TV there is a tremendous range of products from which to choose. Without trade, consumers would have a relatively limited choice, which could reduce their welfare.

6. Trade leads to a **faster rate of technological diffusion**. This leads to the development of better quality products for consumers and enhances their overall standard of living.

Absolute advantage

A country has an **absolute advantage** in the production of a good or service if it can produce that product using fewer factors of production than another nation (that is, more cheaply).

In the example matrix below, production possibilities are shown if two countries each devote 50% of their resources to manufacturing the products shown.

	Tablet Computers	**Smart Phones**
UK	1000	500
Japan	2400	800
Total output	**3400**	**1300**

Japan has an **absolute advantage** over the UK in the production of both tablet computers and smart phones. This is because with an equal amount of resources allocated to both products, Japan can produce more tablet computers than the UK and more smart phones too.

Comparative advantage

Comparative advantage means being able to produce a product at lower **opportunity cost** than other nations.

In the example above, it is possible quickly to see that Japan has a comparative advantage in producing tablet computers, where it is more than twice as efficient than the UK. Japan is less than twice as efficient at producing smart phones. By implication, the UK has a comparative advantage in producing mobile phones.

This can be confirmed by calculating opportunity cost:

● Suppose the UK wished to increase the production of smart phones, the opportunity cost of each extra phone is two tablet computers (1000/500). For Japan, the same decision has an opportunity cost of three tablet computers (2400/800). Therefore, the UK has a comparative advantage in smart phones because it has to give up fewer tablet computers than Japan.

● Suppose Japan wished to increase production of tablet computers, the opportunity cost of one extra tablet computer is $1/3$ of a smart phone (800/2400). For the UK the same decision has an opportunity cost of $1/2$ of a smart phone (500/1000). Thus, Japan has the comparative advantage in tablet computers, because it has to give up fewer smart phones than the UK.

Gains from the trade

Gains from trade are increases in total output occurring as a result of specialisation and trade.

According to the theory of **comparative advantage**, there are possible gains from trade if each country specialises in the product where it has a comparative advantage. This remains true even in our example, where Japan has an absolute advantage in both products.

Suppose the UK now specialises completely in producing smart phones, while Japan allocates 75% of its resources into tablet computers and the remaining 25% into smart phones. The new output levels would be as follows, with a higher output of both products.

Output after specialisation	Tablet Computers	Smart Phones
UK	0	1000
Japan	3600	400
Total output (gain after specialisation)	**3600 (+200)**	**1400 (+100)**

Terms of trade

While we have demonstrated that specialisation can increase world output, how this output is divided between nations depends on the prices at which trade takes place, known as the **terms of trade**.

In our example, the UK can produce smart phones at an opportunity cost of two tablet computers. It will not therefore accept less than two tablets for each smart phone when it trades. Japan has an opportunity cost of three tablet computers for each phone produced domestically. It will therefore not pay more than three tablets for each smart phone it buys from the UK. Thus, for mutually beneficial trade, the terms of trade must lie between the domestic opportunity cost ratios.

For a nation, terms of trade can be summarised as:

Terms of trade = (Index of export prices/index of import prices) x 100.

When a nation's terms of trade increase, this is regarded as an **improvement**. This is because the relative price of its exports has risen and it now has to sell fewer units of exports for each unit of imports it buys. Note, however, that such 'improvements' in terms of trade can happen for undesirable reasons, such as a high rate of inflation relative to other countries.

Assumptions of comparative advantage theory	It is important to remember that the law of comparative advantage is based on a number of underlying assumptions:

- There are **two countries that produce only two goods** – this assumption is made to keep the explanation as simple as possible, but the model can be applied to the world economy where a wide variety of goods and services are produced.

- **Perfect occupational mobility of factors of production** – this means that resources can be easily transferred from smart phone to tablet computer production.

- **Constant returns to scale** (i.e. doubling the input leads to a doubling of output) – it is assumed that the opportunity cost ratios stay constant as resources are transferred from one industry to another. If businesses exploit increasing returns to scale when they specialise, the potential gains from trade are much greater. However, if decreasing returns to scale set in the gains from trade may not materialise.

- **Zero transportation costs** – if we introduce transport costs into the model, then any comparative advantage a country may have could well be eliminated. The implementation of tariffs will have the same effect.

Factors determining comparative advantage	If an economy has a comparative advantage in one good, there is no guarantee that it will last forever. Comparative advantages change all the time. Some countries enjoy a comparative advantage in one product for several years and then lose this advantage when rival producers from other countries enter their markets.

For a country, the following factors are important in determining the relative costs of production and, therefore, comparative advantage:

- **The quantity and quality of factors of production available** – For example, a country with a larger and more skilled workforce is more likely to have a comparative advantage in the production of manufactured goods.

- **Investment in research and development** – may give a nation's firms cost advantages through the development of superior production techniques. R&D may allow a firm to develop products and techniques that it can patent. This will give these firms a significant advantage in the market place.

- **Movements in the exchange rate** – a country with a lower cost of production may not be able to exploit this relative cost advantage fully as the prices of goods and services in international markets are distorted by the exchange rate. For example, a rise in value of a currency will increase the price of exports on international markets. This might eliminate any relative cost advantage.

- **Long term rates of inflation** – if a country has a higher inflation rate than other countries it will lose competitiveness on international markets. As a result, it may lose its comparative advantage in certain areas.

- **Import controls**, such as tariffs, can be used to create an artificial comparative advantage for a country's domestic producers. By raising the price of imports, a government can protect domestic firms from more efficient foreign producers.

- **Non-price competitiveness of producers** – consumers do not just purchase products because they are cheaper than substitutes. Non-price factors such as product design, reliability, quality and after-sales support are also important in determining comparative advantage.

The pattern of trade	The UK's **pattern of trade** refers to:

- How much trade we do (perhaps expressed as a percentage of GDP)?

- Which goods and services we tend to export and which we import?

- Which countries we trade with and how much trade we do with them?

Over time, the UK has tended to trade more. It has imported more manufactured goods and tended to export more services (especially financial services). While America remains a key trading partner, the EU has accounted for an increasing proportion of UK trade. Rapidly developing economies such as China have become increasingly important as a source of UK imports, and more recently exports too.

Competitive-ness

Competitiveness can be defined as the ability of a nation to generate wealth and high standards of living in comparison to other nations. The concept could also be applied to particular regions within a country. The **competitiveness** of countries has become increasingly important as they have become more interconnected through trade as a result of the process known as **globalisation**.

There are a number of distinct aspects to competitiveness, including:

● The **price competitiveness** of a country in international trade. How do prices compare to those of substitute products made in other countries?

● The **non-price competitiveness** of a country in international trade. How do factors such as quality, after-sales service and rates of innovation compare to other countries? A country that is unable to compete effectively on price (e.g. due to relatively high wage costs in comparison to competitor nations) may succeed by differentiating its products or by targeting niche markets. This makes demand for the country's products less elastic, allowing them to command a price premium.

● A diagram to illustrate the effects of non-price competitiveness in shown in Figure 21.1. Suppose that a nation's production costs mean that it cannot match the cheapest world price for a good, shown as P_1. Instead, it charges P_2, but because it is competitive on non-price factors, demand for its product is relatively inelastic (DI) and contracts only to Q_2. Had demand been more elastic (DE) it would have contracted much more, to Q_3.

Figure 21.1: Non-price competitiveness

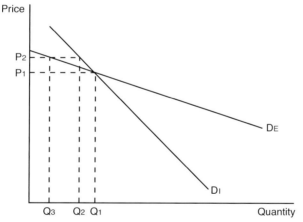

● **The ability of the country to attract Foreign Direct Investment** from multinational companies. Such investment increases productive capacity and can help to produce long-term growth, raising living standards.

● **The ability of the country to produce entrepreneurs** or to attract them from other countries.

● **The ability of the country to attract labour from other nations**, especially highly skilled labour to fill skills gaps. Skills gaps can drive up wages and hence production costs for firms.

Note that the first three bullet points above refer to competitiveness in markets for goods and services. The latter three refer to competitiveness in markets for factors of production.

Floating exchange rates

The process of international trade requires firms and consumers to use different currencies. The **exchange rate** can be defined simply as the price of one currency in terms of another.

Floating exchange rates are determined by the demand and supply of currencies on the foreign exchange markets. The demand and supply of currencies are determined by the following factors:

Demand for a currency	Supply of a currency
• exports of goods	• imports of goods
• exports of services	• imports of services
• inflows of direct investment	• outflows of direct investment
• inflows of portfolio investment and speculative demand for the currency	• outflows of portfolio investment and speculative selling of the currency
• official buying of the currency by the Central Bank	• official selling of the currency by the Central Bank

In Figure 21.2, the equilibrium exchange rate for the pound and the US dollar is at price P, where supply and demand for Sterling are equal.

If there is an **increase in demand** for the pound, due to a surge in exports to the USA, there will be **upward pressure** on the value of the exchange rate. In Figure 21.3, the demand for Sterling will shift to the right from D to D_1 and the value of the pound will appreciate from P to P_1. Conversely, if there is a fall in demand for Sterling, perhaps due to a fall in foreign direct investment from the USA, the demand for Sterling will shift from D to D_2 and the currency will depreciate from P to P_2.

An **increased supply of pounds**, due to a rise in imports from the USA, will apply **downward pressure** on the value of the currency. In Figure 21.4, the supply of Sterling will shift to the right from S to S_1 and the value of the pound will depreciate from P to P_1. Conversely, if there is a fall in supply for Sterling, perhaps due to a fall in speculative selling of the currency, the supply of Sterling will shift from S to S_2 and the currency will appreciate from P to P_2.

Figure 21.2

Figure 21.3

Figure 21.4

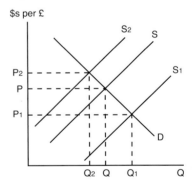

Economic effects of exchange rate movements

A depreciation of Sterling makes UK goods cheaper when priced in a foreign currency. As a result, demand for UK exports should rise, potentially stimulating economic growth and creating employment in the manufacturing and export sectors of the economy, as well as improving the current account of the balance of payments.

However, a weaker exchange rate may be inflationary if it causes demand to be too high, or because it increases the cost of imported raw materials, which may then be reflected in the price of finished products.

Because of the potential advantages of currency depreciation, there is a temptation for governments to manipulate exchange rates in a deliberate attempt to make their currencies weaker. In relation to the current account of the balance of payments, this can be used as an expenditure switching policy to improve the current account position (see Chapter 20). The concepts of the Marshall-Lerner condition and the J-curve are useful in evaluating this policy.

The Marshall-Lerner condition

An **exchange rate depreciation** will not necessarily improve the current account position. An improvement in the current account requires that the value (not volume) of exports rises relative to imports, and whether this occurs depends on the elasticity of demand for exports (ex) and imports (em).

The Marshall-Lerner condition states that a depreciation will improve the current account only if the elasticities of demand for imports and exports sum to greater than one:

ex + em > 1

The J-curve

Elasticity of demand for imports and exports is likely to be low in the short term following a depreciation. This is because importers and exporters are tied in by existing contracts. In the long term, they can adjust to exchange rate changes when new contracts are signed. This means that the current account is likely to deteriorate in the immediate aftermath of an exchange rate depreciation (because the **Marshall-Lerner condition** is not satisfied) but may improve in the longer term when traders have had more chance to react. This produces a **J-curve effect** as shown in Figure 21.5.

Figure 21.5

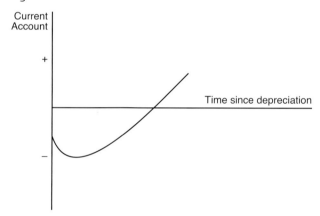

Fixed exchange rate systems

When a country operates a fixed exchange rate, the government loses control over interest rates. Maintaining the exchange rate is likely to require that interest rates be kept broadly in line with those of other countries in the fixed exchange rate system, to prevent flows of **hot money** between countries from putting upward or downward pressure on the exchange rate. Hot money is money which can be moved at short notice in search of a higher interest rate

The need to keep interest rates broadly in line with other countries in the fixed exchange rate system makes it crucial that **convergence** of macroeconomic conditions is achieved between the countries before the fixed rate commences, so that they can tolerate the same interest rate.

Central banks must be willing to add to demand for the domestic currency (by selling foreign exchange reserves) or supply of the currency (buying foreign currency) as needed to preserve the fixed rate.

In Figure 21.6, the equilibrium exchange rate P is below the fixed exchange rate target of P₁. At P₁, there would be an excess supply of the currency. The authorities can shift demand for the currency to D₁ by raising interest rates or buying their own currency using foreign exchange reserves.

Figure 21.6

Advantages and disadvantages of fixed exchange rate systems

Advantages

- A fixed rate can reduce uncertainty for exporters and importers, leading to **trade creation**.

- Greater certainty may help to encourage more investment, leading to economic growth

- A high fixed exchange rate can help to limit demand-pull inflation (exports become less price competitive) and cost-push too (imports, including those of raw materials) become cheaper.

- A low fixed exchange rate can help to boost price competitiveness and hence raise aggregate demand.

Disadvantages

- A fixed rate may make trade with other members of the system artificially cheap relative to that with other trade partners, leading to **trade diversion**.

- Maintaining a fixed rate implies loss of control over interest rates.

- If the economy is in recession, the exchange rate cannot fall to restore its competitiveness.

- History suggests that fixed exchange rates are difficult to maintain (previous fixed rate systems such as the Gold Standard, Bretton Woods and ERM systems have experienced difficulties).

- Speculators may attack a fixed exchange rate if they believe it unrealistic. Sterling was forced out of the ERM in 1992 when it became clear that Sterling's fixed rate was too high and that the UK could not tolerate the high interest rate needed to maintain it.

Hybrid exchange rate systems

These systems exist when governments intervene in foreign exchange markets in order to deliberately weaken or strengthen their currency but do not set a target exchange rate. Such systems are also known as **managed** systems or as '**dirty floating**'. In recent years, the Chinese government have been accused of intervening in foreign exchange markets to weaken the Yuan.

Chapter 22

Paper 2: Measuring the macroeconomy → How the macroeconomy works → Macroeconomic performance → International trade → **Macroeconomic policy tools**

Fiscal policy

Macro-economic policy

This box is repeated at the start of every chapter in the 'Macroeconomic policy tools' section. You are recommended to read it each time.

Macroeconomic policy tools are the instruments at the disposal of the government to help it achieve its main economic objectives: strong, sustainable economic growth, low unemployment, low and stable inflation, a satisfactory position on the current account of the balance of payments.

The main **demand side** policies are **fiscal policy and monetary policy**. We should note, however, that fiscal policy can also be used for supply side purposes. The primary role for demand side policies is to stabilise the economy in the short term, smoothing out the business cycle.

The successful application of demand side policies:

The role of **supply side policy** is to promote the long term health of the economy, boosting the trend growth rate.

The successful application of supply side policies:

| **Fiscal policy** | Fiscal policy involves the use of **government expenditure (G)** and **taxation (T)** to influence the level of **aggregate demand** and also its composition. Fiscal policy can also impact the **supply side** of the economy, for example when it is used to encourage investment or a greater supply of labour. |

Government expenditure

General government expenditure consists of the combined capital and current spending of central and local government including debt interest. It is also known as **public sector spending**, where public sector simply means the government sector of the economy. Note that spending is split into:

● **Current spending** on goods and services – wages of teachers are an example.

● **Capital spending** on investment – building a school is an example.

The biggest categories of government spending in the UK are:

● Social protection – typically around 25% of government expenditure.

● Healthcare – typically a little less than 20% of government expenditure.

● Education – typically around 20% of government expenditure.

Government expenditure is an **injection** into the circular flow of income therefore tends to increase aggregate demand and expand the level of economic activity.

Taxation

A **tax** is any compulsory transfer from a private individual, institution or group to a central or local government. Taxes can be split into:

● **Direct taxes** – Taxes levied on income, wealth and profit. Examples include income tax, national insurance contribution, capital gains tax, council tax and corporation tax.

● **Indirect taxes** – Taxes levied on expenditure. Examples include VAT and excise duties on fuel and alcohol. Road tax is a further example.

Taxation is a **withdrawal** or leakage from the circular flow of income, and therefore tends to cause aggregate demand to fall and the level of economic activity to contract.

Direct taxes, such as income tax, are often **progressive**. This means that the proportion of income paid in tax rises as income rises. In the UK income tax system, this is achieved by a higher **marginal rate of tax** in higher income brackets. A high rate of tax on each extra pound earned beyond a certain level serves to pull up the **average rate of tax** as income rises.

Indirect taxes are seen as **regressive**. This means that the proportion of income paid in tax falls as income rises. A good example of this is the tax on cigarettes. Consider two people who both smoke 20 cigarettes a week. If the tax on a packet of 20 cigarettes is £5, they will both pay the same amount of tax to the government. However, if one of them earns £100 a week and the other £1000 a week, the £5 tax is 5% of the income of the lower earner but only 0.5% for the higher earner. A **regressive tax therefore widens the distribution of income**, which is seen by many as undesirable.

The budget position

The budget position or **fiscal stance** refers to the relative levels of government expenditure (G) and taxation revenue (T). When government spending exceeds taxation revenue there is a **budget deficit**, when the opposite is true there is a **budget surplus**. In summary:

Contractionary stance	**Expansionary stance**
T > G	G > T
Budget surplus	Budget deficit
Government provides net leakages from circular flow	Government provides net injection to circular flow
AD falls and economic activity contracts	AD rises and economic activity expands
Policy **tightening** involves cutting G or raising T	A policy **loosening** involves cutting T or raising G

A budget deficit must be financed by borrowing. The amount that must be borrowed each year to bridge the gap between government expenditure and taxation revenue is known as the **Public Sector Net Cash Requirement** (**PSNCR**). The borrowing needed to finance the budget deficit is a flow which adds to the accumulated **stock** of government debt.

The national debt is the total amount of money owed by the UK government at any one time. If, for example, the national debt is 80% of GDP and the government runs a budget deficit of 5% of GDP in the following year, then the national debt will rise to approximately 85% of GDP. In the event that the government runs a budget surplus, this can be used to repay some of the national debt.

Uses of fiscal policy (1): influencing the level of demand and economic activity

One of the key uses of fiscal policy is to influence the level of aggregate demand.

A **loosening of fiscal policy** such as an increase in government expenditure can be used to **stimulate current economic growth** and **generate employment**. This helps close large output gaps.

A **tightening of policy** may be required to **control demand pull inflation** and **prevent the 'sucking in' of imports** due to high levels of aggregate demand.

In Figure 22.1, there is initially a sizeable output gap, representing spare capacity. An increase in government spending or a cut in taxation (thereby raising disposable income and consumption) is used to stimulate aggregate demand (AD $\rightarrow$ AD$_1$). **National output rises** (Y $\rightarrow$ Y$_1$) and this will generate an increased derived demand for labour **reducing demand deficient unemployment**. It is important to remember that the final change in national output will be greater than the initial stimulus to aggregate demand because of the operation of the **multiplier** process.

Figure 22.1

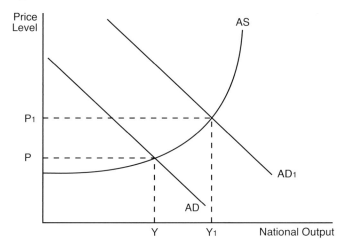

There are, however, potential difficulties with using fiscal policy to stimulate aggregate demand:

- **There is a danger of over stimulating the economy**, leading to inflationary pressure and a deterioration of the current account of the balance of payments. This danger increases as the economy nears full capacity.

- **Governments need knowledge of the size of the output gap and the size of the multiplier** in order to judge how much to increase government expenditure. At best, the output gap and the size of the multiplier can only be estimated.

- **There are time lags involved in fiscal policy changes.** Major changes in fiscal policy are usually only made once a year, following the presentation of the government's budget. The full effects of any fiscal stimulus to AD will only be felt when the multiplier process has run its full course and this could take as long as two years.

- **'Crowding out' may occur.** This is when new government sector activity simply displaces private sector activity. If the government has to borrow to finance expenditure, this may force interest rates up, reducing private sector investment. This reduces the effectiveness of fiscal policy and may be thought undesirable because the government tends to use resources less efficiently than the private sector due to a lack of a profit motive.

Uses of fiscal policy (2): influencing the composition of demand and economic activity

The pattern of spending in a market economy may generate an inefficient allocation of resources (market failure). The government may use fiscal policy to try to **correct some market failures** by encouraging spending on some products and discouraging spending on others:

- **Public goods** such as street lighting and the national defence system would not be provided by the private sector due to the free-rider problem stemming from the non-rivalrous and non-excludable nature of the good. This creates a clear need for government expenditure to fund state provision of the goods concerned.

- **Merit goods** would be provided by the private sector, but not in sufficient quantities. Goods that are associated with positive externalities are often subsidised or provided by the state.

- In contrast, the government may use indirect taxes to discourage the consumption of **demerit goods**, such as alcohol and tobacco, and to deter **polluting activities** that contribute to environmental damage.

Uses of fiscal policy: (3): boosting the supply capacity of the economy

One way of doing this is to use fiscal policy to shift the balance of aggregate demand away from consumption and towards investment. Government may offer tax breaks on profits that firms retain to use for investment purposes, for example. It may cut direct taxes such as income tax and corporation tax in order to provide incentives to work and enterprise.

Uses of fiscal policy (4): the redistribution of income and wealth

Many people consider that the market economy fails to produce equitable outcomes and that a highly unequal distribution of income and wealth is unfair and constitutes a **market failure**.

This justifies government intervention to make the distribution of income and wealth more equal. With regard to income, for example, the UK operates a **progressive taxation system**. This takes a higher proportion of the incomes of high income earners than it does from lower earners. Some of the benefits available through the social security system are only available to those whose incomes are low enough to qualify (**means tested benefits**). Thus fiscal policy is used to redistribute income.

Uses of fiscal policy (5): paying for government

Even in a pure market economy, there are some essential roles for the government such as protecting property rights, preserving the rule of law, issuing currency and so on. Taxation must be levied to pay for the bodies necessary to carry out these roles, such as the police and the courts. There are also a number of regulatory bodies (such as utility regulators like OFGEM) that require financing.

The remaining material in this chapter on fiscal issues is primarily targeted at students of the OCR AS-level specification. Other students will encounter this material in A-level Year 2.

Fiscal issues (1): the consequences of budget deficits and government debt

The following points of evaluation are relevant.

- Budget deficits can have positive impacts on the economy, notably by **stimulating aggregate demand**. The impact on aggregate demand may be boosted by **multiplier effects**, although the multiplier tends to be small in modern economies where there may be a high marginal propensity to import so that much additional spending leaks from the circular flow of income. Keynesian economists believe that budget deficits are appropriate to stimulate economic activity when there is a large **output gap**.

● A number of potential difficulties with using a budget deficit to stimulate AD are covered under 'Uses of fiscal policy (1)'.

● Economists often argue that a cyclical **budget deficit** is not a problem, but a **structural budget deficit** is. A cyclical deficit will be balanced by a budget surplus later on in the economic cycle when the economy is growing more strongly, which generates more taxation revenue and reduces the need for benefit payments. A structural deficit persists regardless of the stage of the business cycle. It is likely to increase during a recession and fall during recovery, but remains present at all times. Running a structural budget deficit is likely to be unsustainable because it implies the need to find more and more sources of funds for the government to borrow.

● Accumulated government debt must be serviced – in other words interest must be paid on it, arguably adding unnecessarily to government spending over time. There are issues of **inter-generational fairness**. Debt accumulated today imposes the need to make future interest rate payments on future tax payers.

● If the government debt becomes very high, doubts may arise about the ability of the government to repay debts when payment becomes due. Debt is normally 'rolled over'; when debts must be repaid, the government does so by borrowing from elsewhere. If there comes a point where the government cannot find anyone to lend this money to it, the government can face **bankruptcy**, or at the very least will have to pay very high interest rates in order borrow more money. This situation has been faced in recent years by some European governments such as that of Greece. The effects are potentially devastating.

● In order to avoid a situation where the government debt becomes unsustainable, measures may have to be taken to reduce budget deficits sharply. Cuts in government spending are known as **austerity measures**. These are often seen as undesirable because cuts to government services or benefits may impact on the living standards of the poorest in society. However, increasing taxes may also be undesirable, for example by reducing **incentives to work** if income tax is raised. Making **efficiency savings** may be a more desirable way to reduce budget deficits where this is possible.

● It is sometimes argued that high levels of government debt are inherently damaging because they **crowd out** the private sector of the economy. This can occur because the government borrowing leaves fewer funds available for private sector firms to borrow in order to invest and grow. By competing for the funds available to borrow, governments may also raise interest rates, this also discouraging private sector investment. Higher taxes to service the government debt may also discourage work and enterprise in the private sector.

Fiscal issues (2): fiscal rules

Fiscal rules are designed to constrain governments in their conduct of fiscal policy. For example, in June 2015, Chancellor George Osborne announced a new rule that governments would be forced to run a budget surplus when the economy is growing. This was an attempt to prevent governments from choosing to run a **structural budget deficit**, a position which is usually seen as sustainable. If economic agents believe that the rule will be followed (is **credible**), this may favourably affect their conduct. Money may be lent to the UK government at lower rates, because there is less risk of the government defaulting on repayments, for example. Further, firms may be more willing to invest if they believe that the government finances are sound enough that it has scope to stimulate the economy in the event of a future downturn.

Fiscal issues (3): what is a good tax?

The starting point for answering this question lies with Adam Smith's canons of taxation. He suggested that a good tax should be:

● **Certain** – The timing and amount should be clearly known to the taxpayer.

● **Convenient** – The means and timing of paying the tax should be convenient to the taxpayer.

- **Cheap to collect** – Cheap to collect as a percentage of the revenue yielded.

- **Equitable** – The amount paid should be fair (it should be related to the ability to pay).

To this list of points a modern economist might add that a good tax should be:

- **Efficient** – Taxes distort economic incentives. For example, income tax can act as a disincentive to work. However, some taxes cause less inefficiency than others (we might regard it as preferable to tax consumption rather than saving, for example) and some can correct inefficiencies (e.g. taxes on demerit goods help to improve resource allocation).

- **Harmonised** with the tax systems of other countries. This is especially important in a single market such as the EU.

In assessing whether a tax is **equitable** there are a number of useful concepts to consider:

- The **ability-to-pay principle** says those with higher incomes should pay more. This may be in absolute terms or as a percentage of income (implying a progressive tax).

- The **benefit principle** suggests that those who receive more services from the government should pay more taxes. This 'you get what you pay for' principle might imply reduced taxes for those who pay for private education or healthcare.

- **Horizontal equity** is concerned with the fair treatment of those whose positions are the same (the same income levels, for example).

- **Vertical equity** is concerned with the fair treatment of individuals whose circumstances are different (such as differences in income).

Fiscal issues (4): evaluating flat rate tax systems

A flat rate tax is neither progressive nor regressive, instead it is **proportional**. An example of a flat rate tax is an income tax system in which each and every pound of income is taxed at 25%, regardless of how much income is earned.

The potential advantages of such a system are:

- **Improved incentives to work.** It can be argued that a progressive tax system discourages work because there are higher marginal rates of tax on high income earners. High income earners may be the most productive workers in an economy, so it is especially important not to discourage them from working.

- **Simplicity.** The system is easy to understand and more simple to administer – this would reduce administration costs.

- **Fairness?** This is an inherently normative concept but some people believe a flat rate tax to be fairer than a progressive system.

The potential disadvantages of a flat rate tax are:

- **Unfairness?** A flat rate tax does not help to redistribute income in the same way as a progressive system. The gap between the post-tax incomes of high and low income earners is likely to grow. This may be seen by many as being unfair.

- A flat rate tax may increase **poverty traps**. At present, some income can be earned tax free or is charged at a relatively low rate of tax. Under a flat rate tax system, low income earners would be charged higher rates of tax than at present. This may make benefits seem a more attractive option in comparison to work at low rates of pay, thus reducing incentives to work for low skilled workers and trapping them in poverty.

Chapter

23

Paper 2: Measuring the macroeconomy → How the macroeconomy works →
Macroeconomic performance → International trade → **Macroeconomic policy tools**

Monetary policy

**Macro-
economic
policy**

**This box is repeated at the start of every chapter in the 'Macroeconomic policy tools'
section. You are recommended to read it each time.**

Macroeconomic policy tools are the instruments at the disposal of the government to help it achieve
its main economic objectives: strong, sustainable economic growth, low unemployment, low and
stable inflation, a satisfactory position on the current account of the balance of payments.

The main **demand side** policies are **fiscal policy and monetary policy**. We should note, however,
that fiscal policy can also be used for supply side purposes. The primary role for demand side policies
is to stabilise the economy in the short term, smoothing out the business cycle.

The successful application of demand side policies:

The role of **supply side policy** is to promote the long term health of the economy, boosting the trend
growth rate.

The successful application of supply side policies:

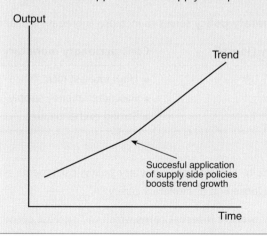

Monetary policy

Monetary policy can be used to influence aggregate demand and inflation. It covers the following **policy instruments**:

- **Interest rates**
- **The money supply**
- **The exchange rate**

In general, interest rates measure the **rate of return on savings** and the **cost of borrowed money**. There is clearly more than one interest rate in the economy. Secured loans (such as mortgages – the house can be repossessed if the borrower fails to meet repayments) carry a lower rate of interest than unsecured personal loans, which carry a greater risk to the lender. Credit cards carry a high rate of interest. This is the price the borrower pays for 'borrowing on demand'. Financial intermediaries such as banks and building societies charge higher rates to borrowers than they do to savers. However, the government (or the central bank on its behalf – the Bank of England in the UK) sets the official **base rate** for the economy and this influences other interest rates.

There is no single definition of the money supply but, as well as notes and coins in circulation, it includes deposits that are available to be spent such as those in the current account of bank customers. Banks are able to add to the money supply by creating deposits when they make loans to customers.

The exchange rate is the price of one currency in terms of another, determined by the demand and supply of currencies on the foreign exchange markets.

Contrac-tionary and expansionary monetary policies

When monetary policy is used to restrict aggregate demand it is known as a **contractionary or tight monetary policy**.

The three elements of a tight monetary policy are a high interest rate, a restricted money supply and a strong exchange rate. In practice these three components are linked. A high interest rate tends to restrict the growth of the money supply because there is a lower demand for loans and this restricts the ability of banks to create new deposits. A high interest rate also strengthens the exchange rate by encouraging a higher demand for the currency from those living overseas who wish to earn a high interest rate on their money.

An **expansionary** or **loose monetary policy** serves to increase aggregate demand.

Expansionary monetary policy (loose)	Contractionary monetary policy (tight)
• Low interest rate	• High interest rate
• Money supply allowed to grow	• Restricted money supply
• Weak exchange rate	• Strong exchange rate

Monetary policy instruments

Students are expected to be able to explain how monetary policy instruments affect the economy. The examples provided here are for a loosening of monetary policy:

A **lower base rate** leads to lower **market interest rates** which will increase consumption. This is because there will be: (i) a fall in saving, as the opportunity cost of spending has fallen; (ii) an increase in demand for consumer durables purchased on credit, as loan repayments fall; (iii) a rise in discretionary incomes, as falling mortgage repayments increase the ability of homeowners to spend. Lower market interest rates may also lead to a rise in investment.

A weaker exchange rate makes UK exports more competitive, and reduces the attractiveness of imports to UK consumers (making them more likely to buy domestically). This causes a rise in net exports, a component

Quantitative easing is carried out by the Bank of England creating new money which it uses to buy bonds from financial institutions such as banks.

of aggregate demand. A weaker exchange rate also increases the cost of imported raw materials, which may eventually feed through to higher consumer prices and inflation.

A growing money supply stimulates AD. Increases in the money supply can be deliberately engineered through **quantitative easing**. This is commonly seen as an **unconventional policy** to be used when the base rate of interest is already very low and there is little scope to cut it further.

Quantitative easing is carried out by the central bank (the Bank of England) creating new money which it uses to buy **bonds** from financial institutions such as banks. A bond is issued by the government when it borrows money and is confirmation of the debt which the government owes to the bond holder.

Quantitative easing may stimulate aggregate demand through a number of channels such as:

● Banks give up bonds in exchange for cash. They now have greater liquidity which increases the availability of credit to consumers and loans to firms who wish to invest.

● With more funds available to lend, the interest rates (**market interest rates**) charged when lending takes place may fall.

● The government pays a fixed amount of interest annually to bond holders. When the central bank buys bonds, it forces their prices up, and the fixed interest payment is now a lower percentage of the price of the bond. This encourages savers to buy other assets such as shares or houses in preference to buying bonds, because savers typically seek the best rate of return they can get on their money. Asset prices may rise across the economy, boosting wealth and confidence, which in turn leads to greater consumption.

Central banks

The central bank is the national bank, in the UK's case the Bank of England. Central banks have a number of responsibilities including:

● Issuing currency.

● Overseeing the banking system.

- Providing banking services to the government.

- Providing banking services to the country's commercial banks.

- Implementing monetary policy on behalf of the government.

Objectives and targets of monetary policy

An **expansionary monetary policy** is typically used to **stimulate economic growth** by **boosting aggregate demand**, although drawbacks include the danger of demand pull inflation and the 'sucking in' of imports as consumer spending increases. A contractionary monetary policy is used to control inflation.

The primary target of UK monetary policy is currently to meet the inflation target of 2% inflation as measured by the rate of change of the Consumer Price Index.

The benefit of **inflation targeting** is that it may establish **credibility**, such that economic agents come to expect low and stable inflation. Benefits of this include:

- Low pay settlements are more likely, preventing **wage-price spirals**.

- Low and stable inflation also gives firms the confidence to invest

However, there are also disadvantages of inflation targeting:

- If inflation appears under control, interest rates can remain low for long periods of time. This may allow dangerous **bubbles** to develop in asset markets. House price inflation may be too rapid, for example. If this later gives way to a housing market crash, the macroeconomy may be severely damaged.

- Sometimes the base rate of interest must be kept high in order to control inflation, even though this damages economic growth. Some economists believe that it may be more appropriate to target a particular rate of economic growth rather than a particular rate of inflation.

The UK framework for monetary policy established by the Bank of England Act 1998 allows that monetary policy can be used to support growth, but only where this is compatible with meeting the 2% inflation target.

The Monetary Policy Committee

It has nine members, five from the Bank of England (including the Governor of the bank) and four outside experts. It meets monthly to decide on the base rate of interest as well as any other relevant policy measures such as quantitative easing.

Inflation must be kept within 1% either side of the 2% inflation target, so within a range of 1-3%. Failure to keep inflation within this range results in the Governor of the Bank writing an open (published) letter to the Chancellor of the Exchequer explaining why meeting the target has not been possible. Policy decisions are taken on the basis of a majority vote amongst the nine members of the committee and the minutes of monthly meetings are published.

Thus the Monetary Policy Committee in general and the Governor in particular are **accountable** for meeting the inflation target.

Setting the base rate

When the MPC sets the base rate, it takes into account a number of factors. It is often argued that changes to the base rate take around 18-24 months to have their full impact on the economy. The MPC must therefore be forward looking trying to build up a picture of what will be happening in the economy over the next two years in order to judge the appropriate base rate to set.

Factors taken into account by the MPC when setting interest rates include:

Demand and output

The key factor to be considered is the likely strength of demand compared to economic capacity in the medium term, so that a judgement about the size of the output gap can be reached. A large negative output gap puts downward pressure on inflation and thus could justify low interest rates. Indicators that might be taken into account include:

- Retail sales data
- Consumer confidence surveys
- Business investment intentions surveys
- Housing market data
- Government spending and taxation
- The trade balance
- Growth of GDP in comparison to trend

Costs and prices

Increases in costs can be passed along the supply chain with the prices of raw materials and factors of production affecting the prices charged by manufacturers which then affect prices charged to consumers. In effect, there may be an inflation 'pipeline' with cost increases at the beginning of the supply chain later coming through as consumer price inflation, although some of any increase in costs may be absorbed by firms at various stages of the chain. Indicators to take into account include:

- Commodity prices (such as oil)
- 'Factory gate prices' (prices charged by firms to wholesalers)
- Exchange rates (affect prices of imported raw materials)
- Wage increases
- Unemployment (may affect future wage settlements)
- Labour productivity (along with wages, determines unit labour costs)
- Changes to expenditure taxes
- Transport costs
- Trends in consumer prices in key sectors of the economy, such as food and domestic energy prices

The international economy

Events in the international economy are increasingly important to UK economic performance. Exports are an important source of demand for UK products, while events in the international economy can deliver shocks that have large effects on our own economy. Indicators to consider include:

- Growth and economic performance in the EU
- Growth and economic performance in the USA
- Growth and economic performance in emerging economies such as China
- Global growth forecasts from bodies such as the International Monetary Fund (IMF)
- International threats such as crisis in the Eurozone

Financial markets

Data from financial markets can give important clues as to what is happening in an economy. For example, buoyant asset prices may feed through to higher consumption through wealth effects, or may later give way to asset price crashes which can severely dampen growth. Indicators to consider include:

- Share prices
- Market interest rate data (market interest rates such as mortgage rates may be affected by the base rate but depend on other factors too)
- Exchange rates
- Bond yields (which affect the cost of government borrowing)

Chapter

24

Paper 2: Measuring the macroeconomy → How the macroeconomy works →
Macroeconomic performance → International trade → **Macroeconomic policy tools**

Supply side policies – can policy conflicts and trade-offs be resolved?

Macro-economic policy

This box is repeated at the start of every chapter in the 'Macroeconomic policy tools' section. You are recommended to read it each time.

Macroeconomic policy tools are the instruments at the disposal of the government to help it achieve its main economic objectives: strong, sustainable economic growth, low unemployment, low and stable inflation, a satisfactory position on the current account of the balance of payments.

The main **demand side** policies are **fiscal policy and monetary policy**. We should note, however, that fiscal policy can also be used for supply side purposes. The primary role for demand side policies is to stabilise the economy in the short term, smoothing out the business cycle.

The successful application of demand side policies:

The role of **supply side policy** is to promote the long term health of the economy, boosting the trend growth rate.

The successful application of supply side policies:

Supply side policies	Supply side policies are policies that aim to:

- **increase productivity**
- **improve incentives** and
- **improve the efficiency of resource allocation** in order to **boost the trend growth rate** (potential growth) of the economy and shift the aggregate supply curve to the right.

A distinctive feature of supply side policies is that they usually involve reducing the role of the government in the economy. Supply side policies are thus usually **market orientated** policies that reflect a belief that the private sector of the economy uses resources more efficiently than the public (government) sector. However, a minority of supply side policies are interventionist, enlarging the role of government. Compulsory education is an example.

It is important to remember that the trend (potential) growth rate of the economy reflects the rate at which the economy's capacity grows and that capacity is a function of the quantity and quality of the four factors of production: land, labour, capital and enterprise.

Figure 24.1 shows the effects of the successful application of supply side policies.

Figure 24.1

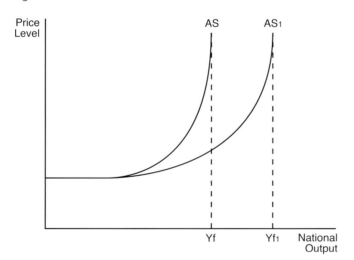

We should also note that not all **supply side improvements** come about through government policy. Many are introduced by private sector firms, for example, new workplace practices and production methods that improve efficiency.

(1) Labour market policies	Supply side policies in the labour market aim to improve the skills of the labour force (**human capital**), promote **labour mobility**, **remove barriers** that prevent wages reaching equilibrium levels and encourage **flexible working practices** (part-time work, shift work, temporary contracts) that help control costs of production. Specific examples include:

- Income tax cuts to improve incentives to work.

- Cuts in benefit payments to make voluntary unemployment less affordable.

- Tax relief on income earned from renting out accommodation. The rented housing sector promotes labour mobility.

- Removal of the national minimum wage so that the labour market can reach equilibrium.

- Measures to reduce the power of trade unions.

● Reduced government regulation of labour markets to lower the non-wage costs of taking on workers.

● Financial help for firms that invest in the training of workers.

● Changes to the education system to broaden access to further and higher education and to promote vocational training.

(2) Product market policies

Product market policies aim to offer encouragement to private sector firms and to promote competition. Examples include:

● Privatisation, such as the sale of state owned firms to private shareholders.

● Deregulation of markets to open them up to new competition. This occurred in the UK gas and electricity markets, which were at one time statutory monopolies with a single supplier.

● Tax relief on profits retained by firms for investment purposes.

(3) Policies in financial markets

It is important that firms have access to finance in order to invest and innovate. Supply side policies in this area focus on making finance more readily available. One example in the UK was the creation of the Alternative Investment Market (AIM) to allow firms not yet ready to be listed on the Stock Exchange to raise share capital.

(4) Policies to encourage enterprise

Policies to encourage enterprise include:

● Low corporation tax, to increase the profit incentive and stimulate investment.

● Reduced regulation of business. The rules imposed on business by government are sometimes known as 'red tape' and the aim of supply side policies would be to reduce these bureaucratic requirements. Even the length of time to go through the administrative processes of starting up a company can vary widely from country to country.

● Patents to allow those who innovate to exploit the commercial potential of their ideas free from competition for an initial period of time.

The UK gas and electricity markets were at one time statutory monopolies with a single supplier.

Policy trade-offs and conflicts

Policy conflicts often exist when the government tries to achieve its objectives. This is particularly true when demand side policies are used. Brief details of these conflicts are given in Chapter 15. There may be **trade-offs** such that achieving one policy objective makes others more difficult to obtain. Specific examples of trade-offs include:

Conflict/trade-off	Detail
Growth and inflation	Higher levels of aggregate demand (AD) are necessary for the short run growth of the economy. However, as AD increases, the spare capacity in the economy is used and the output gap closes. Firms may have the confidence to raise prices given that the level of demand is high relative to available output. Thus demand-pull inflation may result.
Unemployment and inflation	As unemployment falls (due, for example, to higher levels of AD and thus a higher derived demand for labour), firms may experience labour shortages, especially of skilled workers. They may raise wages in an attempt to attract the workers they need. Higher wages increase the spending power of workers but also raise the costs of firms. Both may cause inflation. The unemployment-inflation trade-off is shown in the **short run Phillips curve** (see right):
Inflation and the balance of payments	A strong exchange rate can be useful in controlling inflation. This is because a strong currency makes exports more expensive and imports cheaper, thereby limiting net exports and constraining aggregate demand. The strong currency also makes imported raw materials cheaper, helping to control cost-push inflation. However, by making exports less competitive and imports more attractive, a strong currency may damage the current account of the balance of payments.
Growth and the balance of payments	The achievement of economic growth is associated with an increase in consumer and investment spending. Some of this spending is inevitably import expenditure (the extent depending on the marginal propensity to import). Higher import expenditure leads to a deterioration of the current account of the balance of payments.
Growth and income inequality	The benefits of economic growth are often shared unequally, with high income earners gaining more than those with low incomes. Indeed, some policies designed to promote economic growth, such as cutting higher rates of income tax to improve incentives to work for the most productive workers, may directly contribute to inequality.

Resolving policy conflicts

Supply side improvements offer the potential to resolve many of the policy conflicts outlined in the previous section. It is often held that the fundamental long term performance of the economy is determined by the health of its supply side.

Supply side improvements may potentially lead to simultaneous improvements in all of the four main economic indicators. Boosting economic capacity is associated with long-run growth of GDP, which may create an increased derived demand for labour and reduce unemployment, for example. The increase in capacity should serve to reduce inflationary pressure, which in turn makes domestically produced output more competitive on international markets. Some of the increased capacity can thus serve export markets, allowing for an improvement on the current account of the balance of payments.

No long run trade-offs according to classical economists

Classical economists argue that any trade-offs between objectives may exist only in the short run.

The short and long run version of AS makes the point that there may be no trade-off between economic objectives in the long run as it is assumed that the markets for factors of production adjust to ensure full employment of all resources.

Even if an increase in AD stimulated output and employment in the short term, its long run effect is purely inflationary and it may also lead to a deterioration of the current account of the balance of payments. Shifts of the LRAS are likely to lead to simultaneous improvement or deterioration in all four main indicators, as explained in the previous section on resolving policy conflicts.

No long run trade-offs between economic objectives

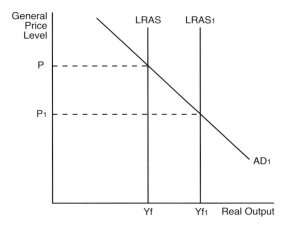

An increase in AD **fails** to increase output and reduce unemployment in the **long run**, **but** is inflationary and is likely to lead to a deterioration of the current account of the balance of payments.

An increase in LRAS is likely to improve all four main economic indicators simultaneously.

Evaluating supply side policies

The chief benefit of supply side policies is that they may improve the fundamental long term performance of the economy, increasing its competitiveness in relation to other economies. Supply side policies have the potential to resolve conflicts between policy objectives as explained in the preceding sections.

However:

● Supply side improvements are not easy to achieve. After years of supply side reforms, UK labour productivity still lags behind other leading nations such as the USA and Germany, for example.

● Time-lags are involved and supply side policies are typically not quick in having an effect on the economy.

● Supply side policies may not be an appropriate response to cyclical problems such as recessions. This is because the fundamental problem here may be a short term lack of demand. Market-based reforms may then not tackle the problem, although arguably some interventionist supply side policies such as increased spending on infrastructure would help.

● Supply side reforms, despite resolving some policy conflicts, may introduce a new one. Some supply side measures, such as reductions in trade union power and abolishing minimum wages, leave workers vulnerable. They are argued by some to cause a lack of equity, despite enhancing the efficiency of the economy. They thus contribute to an **equity-efficiency trade-off**.